COOKING with
CORY

COOKING with CORY

Inspirational Recipes for the Fearless Cook

CORY PARSONS

whitecap

Whitecap Books is known for its expertise in the cookbook market, and has produced some of the most innovative and familiar titles found in kitchens across North America. Visit our website at www.whitecap.ca.

Edited by Elaine Jones
Interior design and typesetting by Setareh Ashrafologhalai
Food photography by Lance Sullivan / Concept Photography
Photo assistance by Rainer Plendl
Photography on pages ii (bottom right), 7, 30 (bottom), and 43 (bottom left) by Michelle Furbacher
Food styling by Cory Parsons

Printed in Canada at Friesens

Library and Archives Canada Cataloguing in Publication

Parsons, Cory, 1974–
    Cooking with Cory : inspirational recipes for the fearless cook / Cory Parsons.

Includes index.
ISBN 978-1-77050-022-8

    1. Cookery. I. Title.

TX714.P3755 2010   641.5   C2010-904311-1

The publisher acknowledges the financial support of the Government of Canada through the Canada Book Fund (CBF) and the Province of British Columbia through the Book Publishing Tax Credit.

10 11 12 13 14   5 4 3 2 1

ENVIRONMENTAL BENEFITS STATEMENT

Whitecap Books Ltd saved the following resources by printing the pages of this book on chlorine free paper made with 10% post-consumer waste.

TREES	WATER	SOLID WASTE	GREENHOUSE GASES
10 FULLY GROWN	**4,693** GALLONS	**285** POUNDS	**975** POUNDS

Calculations based on research by Environmental Defense and the Paper Task Force.
Manufactured at Friesens Corporation

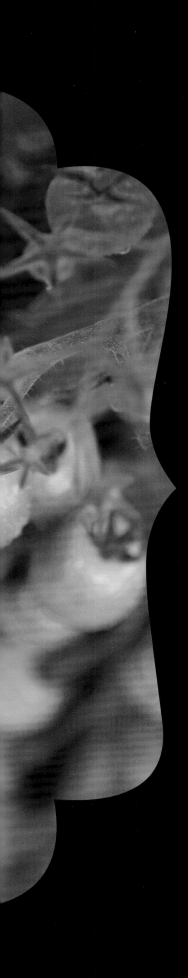

Contents

Foreword

I first met Cory Parsons while working as the personal training manager for a local fitness centre in Nanaimo, British Columbia. We hadn't really gotten to know one another, other than through general passing conversation. The day I heard the news of his accident and that he had been paralyzed, I was struck by how quickly life can change. When Cory returned to the gym, we were unsure what to say when we saw him. Cory just smiled and said, "I'm back." He went out of his way to make us feel comfortable with his situation. Incredible! After talking for a bit, Cory lamented jokingly that he had just recently bought a new pair of roller blades and wondered what he was going to do with them now.

It was nothing short of amazing to witness the following months. If there was a time when Cory felt sorry for himself, he never showed it. Day after day he showed up and pushed his body as hard as he could. Whatever limitations the medical professionals told him he would have as a result of his accident, he did everything he could to prove them wrong.

I'm so impressed by Cory's strong spirit—from getting back to the gym to competing in a natural bodybuilding show to being an author of an inspirational cookbook. Being in a wheelchair has only strengthened Cory's resolve to make a positive impact on the world around him. Funny how those we first sought to inspire can end up inspiring us right back.

—David Gilks

David Gilks is the medical exercise program director of Core Essentials, a personal training and rehabilitation centre in Nanaimo, British Columbia.

Introduction

MY STORY

I was born in 1974 in the small town of Kitimat, on the west coast of Canada. I was a rambunctious and adventurous kid, often getting myself into trouble of some kind. After moving to Vancouver Island in 1988, to another small British Columbia town—Nanaimo—I found myself growing up very quickly. I moved out on my own at the age of 16, still in high school, and needed to work to support my independence. At that age my employment options were limited, but I found work in the restaurant industry, and I loved the fast-paced, social environment. I've always been fond of cooking and eating, and I felt very much at home when I was working hard to make and serve the very best food I could.

At 20 years old I made the decision to pack up my belongings and travel throughout Europe for at least a year. This trip expanded my culinary palate and broadened my views on culture, religion, and life in general. When the year was up, I moved back to Nanaimo and started working in—you guessed it—the food service industry. It was still a natural fit, and I was quite successful.

Every summer I would ride my motorcycle to Kelowna, in the interior of British Columbia, to visit my mother and enjoy Thunderfest. This was a waterfront extravaganza where the main feature was the hydroplane boat races, but so many people attended for the fantastic social environment—food, music, people. It was there in 1997 that I met the woman of my dreams. We made eye contact; no words were spoken, but it was the type of attraction that takes your breath away and makes every hair on your body tingle. We met at a small bar later that evening and danced all night long—into the streets, and onto the beach—until the sun came up. You could almost see the sparks flying like fireworks in the night, and I knew that this woman would change my life forever.

I was in love! It was the maddening, crazy, and complete-and-utter-surrendering type of love. We lived in different provinces but corresponded by phone over the following year. We made plans to rendezvous in Kelowna on the one-year anniversary of the day we first met. The anticipation of that day kept me awake at night for weeks. True to our word, we met one year later. She was finally in my arms again and I was happy. This was the beginning of the best and worst period of my life.

After enjoying the waterfront festivities, completely lovestruck and a little intoxicated, we decided to go for a quick swim before returning to my mother's house for dinner. I should point out that I was an ego-driven, 23-year-old male showing off for his new sweetheart. Lost in the excitement, I dove into shallow water and my head hit the bottom, crushing the bones in my neck.

Immediately I knew I had done something very serious—I was completely paralyzed from the chin down. I needed desperately to breathe but was unable to reach the surface. Fortunately for me, my love was a registered nurse and recognized the severity of what had happened. Without waiting a second, she swam to me and pulled me from the water, reassuring me that everything was going to be okay. She was an angel who had come into my life to rescue me from certain death.

Unfortunately, the waterfront rescue team was not adequately experienced in spinal rescue, and to make things worse, the person who had just saved my life was pulled away from me. Lying

on the hot concrete waiting for an ambulance, I watched my angel but could not believe what I was seeing; she was sobbing into her hands and being gently held in the arms of a priest in his full habit. I have never considered myself a religious man, but I can tell you honestly that at that moment I was praying it was all a bad dream, and that I would wake up. But it wasn't a dream; it was a nightmare from which I would never wake. My life was changed forever.

LIFE-CHANGING PROGNOSIS

At the hospital there was no mistaking the severity of my injury. The x-rays showed a complete destruction and dislocation of the sixth vertebra in my neck. The doctor told me that not only would I never walk again but that this type of injury meant I would be a quadriplegic for the rest of my life. At this point my understanding of quadriplegia was very limited—I thought I would have to blink once for yes and twice for no for the rest of my life. I looked into his eyes and, still barely able to speak, begged him to kill me because I didn't think I would ever be able to live a life under those conditions.

Obviously he didn't oblige me, for which I am very grateful because since that day I have gone on to find great happiness and fulfillment.

Although I am classified as "a quadriplegic confined to a wheelchair," I can do so much more than blink, and do not feel confined to anything. I do not have voluntary motor function of my hands or fingers, but do have mobility in my arms, shoulders, and head.

MY FIRST CHALLENGE

After surgery to stabilize the bones in my neck, I was sent to a rehabilitation hospital to learn how to deal with my new body. My angel was there with me and she even took employment in the hospital, working with surgeons who perform spinal surgery on others like me.

On my first day of occupational therapy at the rehab hospital, I was faced with my greatest challenge. I was sitting at a table, and a therapist placed an orange in front of me and asked me to pick it up. Sounds simple, right? It sounded simple to me, but remember, my hands didn't work and my mind was full of questions. *If I can't pick it up, then what? If I'm not able to pick up this orange, then how am I supposed to survive and become independent?*

It wasn't until I had asked myself *how* I was going to pick it up that I actually started the problem-solving process. The transition between *Can I do this?* and *How am I going to get this done?* was where I began to take action. I attempted various methods, repeatedly dropping my orange on the floor and having to ask for help each time. After nearly an hour of sheer perseverance, I finally had my orange! I was victorious! Invincible! Through determination and persistence I had triumphed over this, my greatest obstacle.

I told my family and friends of this great success, but they didn't seem to appreciate its significance in the same way that I did. Picking up an orange isn't a great accomplishment, after all, and it wasn't until I had told my fellow patients of my victory that I was greeted with the accolades I felt I deserved. Other patients in the hospital would look to me and say, "I can't do that," and I would answer, "Yes you can! I just did it, and I'll show you."

NEVER GIVE UP

My situation has been described in many ways: disabled, paralyzed, person with a disability, handicapped. I don't feel I can be summed up by any of these terms. In fact, I see myself as "handy-capable," and I hope you can share this vision with me.

My hand is up, not out. I am not someone looking for sympathy or pity: I'm a person who is hoping to motivate, educate, relate to, and inspire others who have disabilities (the "handy-capable") and anyone else who might feel limited by their own lack of ability. What about you? You might have no idea how to cook, or you might feel you haven't had success when you've tried, but it doesn't mean you are destined for failure. It simply means that you are still learning. Mistakes are only lessons from which you have not yet learned.

Occasionally it is necessary to look back at where you've been to discover just how far you've come. I can proudly say now that I have come a long way and look forward to seeing just how far I can go. The past ten years of my life are evidence that my injury has not caused me to give up on my dreams. In fact, my injury may have encouraged me to try even harder. I don't know anyone who gets it right every time. I've found through my own lessons that I learned a lot more from getting it wrong than from getting it right. This book is proof of the many lessons I have learned.

Since my injury I have participated in my first bodybuilding competition and gone hang-gliding (a lifelong ambition). And in 2009, for the very first time in history, a quadriplegic participated in the World Championship Bathtub Race, held right here in Nanaimo, British Columbia. Who was this person? Me, of course! Currently, through motivational speaking and setting a healthy example, I am working hard to inspire others to realize their goals.

I consider this cookbook my proverbial orange, and the determination and hard work it has taken to create it has been of great satisfaction to me. I started this project in order to showcase the limitless possibilities for people with disabilities. I wanted to show that we all have the opportunity to achieve and excel.

In the hospital I was told that one day I would be able to cook, drive, and take care of myself independently. But at that time I was completely dependent on others. As I was being fed three meals a day, I could not comprehend, even in my wildest dreams, how I would one day do it on my own. But I was inspired to find out if what they were saying really was possible. If I had to live this life, I was going to do the very best I could. The part of my personality that had embraced life before the accident once again emerged to fight for that vision of the future.

This inspiration was something I found necessary to share with others who were in similar situations, and I thought, *I'm not going to tell you, I'm going to show you!* My mantra, "Yes, you can," is best represented by this cookbook. It took a lot of trial and error, frustrating failures, and new learning. I wasn't sure what my potential was—and I'm still not, as I progress in this life from day to day. But I knew in my heart that if I was willing to try I would eventually succeed. It has never been a matter of *if* but simply *how*.

WHO IS THIS BOOK FOR?

This book is for everyone who enjoys cooking and eating delicious food. We all must eat every day but this doesn't mean our food needs to be mundane or bland. In fact, each meal is another opportunity to experience something amazing.

Food has the power to influence us on many levels. Not only does what we choose to eat have an effect on our senses—how it smells, looks, tastes, and feels—but it also affects our health and determines how we power our body and soul.

Even with a severe disability such as quadriplegia, I have had wonderful experiences and have gained a sense of my own independence, and the opportunity to share my culinary creations in this book has given me great happiness. I have always dreamed big. I have always lived hard. Cooking is something I can share with the world, and for me it is a real passion.

I hope *Cooking with Cory* inspires you to reach for your dreams, whatever they may be. We all have a special talent. Whether you are disabled or able-bodied, an experienced cook or a beginning chef, this book is tangible evidence that those dreams can come true. All you need is a willingness to try.

COOKING FOR OTHERS

I love sharing food and entertaining. Whether you're a beginner cook or an accomplished chef, this book gives you recipes that you can make and enjoy with those you love. I encourage people of all skill levels and abilities to experience the joy that entertaining brings to themselves and to their family and friends.

Cooking for others can sometimes be intimidating, especially if you've invited a guest with cooking experience, or if you're trying something adventurous. I find it thrilling to challenge myself and attempt variations on successful dishes. The trick here is to have fun: enjoy the process and you won't worry so much about the outcome.

We've all heard the saying, "Life is a journey, not a destination." The same holds true in the kitchen. Rarely do I make a dish exactly the same way twice. Aside from baking, where ingredients and measurements must be exact, cooking is open to interpretation and provides the opportunity to experiment and create your own twist on a signature dish. I see recipes as guidelines, not rules, and sometimes breaking the rules can be fun!

I take great satisfaction when people ask, "What is that special flavour?" or say, "I taste something unique." I love creating a dish that is recognizable to the eye, but is a complete surprise to the palate.

THE FOOD WE EAT

Healthy, fresh, sustainable ingredients are key to wonderful food. If it looks good before you even begin to cook, you're well on your way to a successful dining experience. If those ingredients are from an organic garden right outside your back door, nothing could be fresher or more flavourful and healthy. The best part is, if you run out of something in the kitchen, your produce market is merely steps away!

So many of the foods that we consume today are grown in sterile environments and are completely devoid of nutrients and minerals, not to mention that pesticides and chemicals can often leave a toxic residue. Even those who have gardens can't grow everything they need, but purchasing from local growers is another way to support our communities. As a gardener, I often have more produce than I'm able to consume, and so I share with my neighbours and in return they share with me. It is a fundamental way of creating a sense of belonging within your community.

Organic gardening, and gardening in general, has been a rewarding part of my life since I was a child. My father has a green thumb, and although I protested picking the rocks and weeds then, I have reaped some benefits as an adult. The experience of planting tiny seeds and watching them grow, and then consuming the fruits of your labour, is magical. Using this superior produce in dishes I create is, for me, ultimate enjoyment.

Since my injury I've been interviewed by BCTV, who asked why I enjoy gardening. My response was, "Because I can." Gardening is another area where I've been able to realize my potential as a disabled person and take on responsibility with passion in my "new" life. Making my garden accessible has been a simple matter of using large planters and raised garden beds. I have had amazing results, and each year is more rewarding than the last.

DIVERSE DISHES

As you read over these recipes, it is going to become very clear that they vary greatly in their origins and ingredients. These dishes have been influenced by my family, my culinary experiences here in Nanaimo, and my travels in North Africa. The year I spent in Europe tasting local delicacies and sampling traditional dishes also made a lasting impression on me.

It was my intention to see the sights of a city and then move into the outlying areas to experience the local culture from the perspective of someone interested in learning and preserving what makes each country so unique from a cultural and culinary standpoint. Now, I have recipes for amazing curry dishes, even though I didn't visit India. In fact, I had the best curry of my life in England and I've heard it said that a better curry there will never be. And here in North Amercia we can share in the specialties of many different culinary backgrounds.

I hope I have imparted a taste of my life's journey through these recipes. My personal preference leads me to the exotic and spicy, as I have found that a little sweet heat brings out flavour in food that might otherwise have gone unnoticed. So next time you are making a dish, don't be afraid to take a trip and try something reminiscent of another country. Bon appétit!

HEALTH & WELLNESS

As a young, active man, I had always been interested in athletics and nutrition. Whether I was participating in competitive sports or monitoring my own personal health, nutrition was a major consideration in my success. After my injury, I made a transition from extreme athlete to somebody who sat around a lot, and that had huge repercussions for my diet and my health.

The importance of good health and nutrition cannot be overstated, especially when it comes to people who live a sedentary lifestyle in wheelchairs. We simply can't afford to be overweight because of the strain it puts on our bodies and the increased difficulty it causes in getting around.

But just because we have to watch our weight and eat as healthy a diet as possible does not mean we have to sacrifice great taste.

Moderation has often been defined by excess, and I have learned this the hard way. Several years ago I was very overweight and extremely unhappy. Although I was maintaining an active lifestyle, I was not monitoring my diet responsibly and the consequences began to affect my everyday life. It gradually became more difficult to maintain my independence and I began to feel I was not only not moving forward, but actually taking steps backward in my recovery.

We are all responsible for the decisions we make in our lives, and we are the only ones who can create change. Accepting this fact was the first step to improving my health and well-being. From there, I began educating myself on what a proper diet would look like for somebody with my activity level and body fat percentage. With a new diet, in a very short time I was feeling better, looking better, and realizing the benefits of the hard work I was putting in at the gym. Within one year I'd gone from nearly 200 pounds at 15 percent body fat to a very respectable 160 pounds at 7 percent body fat.

The transition was so amazing that I wanted to share my success story with others through motivational speaking and the recipes contained in this health-conscious cookbook. The components of a healthy lifestyle must be cohesive in order to achieve the desired goals. Moderation is certainly the key; it is as simple as calories in versus calories out, so your activity level determines just how often you can visit the snack cupboard. Overindulgence will lead to being overweight. I look at it in terms of earning a treat or reward for my hard work, and the harder I work, the less likely I am to have an unhealthy snack.

Moderation, education, and good old-fashioned hard work are my recommendations for a successful journey to a healthier and happier lifestyle: they will ensure you have the best chance of reaching your goals and dreams. That, and cooking with the healthy recipes in this book!

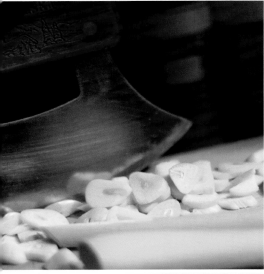

COOKWARE

My desire to get into the kitchen was not diminished after my injury, although some adaptations were necessary for my safety and to accommodate my abilities. You might imagine that someone who is quadriplegic *and* working with sharp knives would be absolutely frightening! Well, that's only your imagination. In reality, with practice and determination I have become quite skilled in the kitchen. The adaptations to my kitchen include lowered countertops, plenty of room to maneuver my chair, and an array of carefully chosen kitchen utensils.

Ulu

Through trial and error I have discovered that an ulu style of knife works very well for those with limited hand function. The design of its handle helps me keep good contact and maintain control. Chopping and slicing is made easy with just a simple rocking motion. I now own three of them because I like them to stay sharp, and this allows me to rotate them as each one gets dull. Sharpening can be done at many knife shops, and sharpening stones are sold at most hardware stores. It's really important to purchase an ulu made with good-quality steels since a sharp knife also allows for greater control and therefore increased safety. You can purchase ulus in specialty cooking stores or online. (Try www.ulu.com.)

Can Opener

Occasionally while cooking, the need to open a can will arise. I've discovered a battery-operated can opener to help me overcome this obstacle (since I have limited hand mobility); it's called One-Touch. As its name suggests, one simple touch and the opener does the work for you. It's available at most kitchen stores and some hardware stores as well.

Pots & Pans

The Jamie Oliver line of cookware has some features that I find very useful in the kitchen. The handles stay cool, which can help prevent accidental burns. The rubber inserts under the handles improve grip, and this aids in control especially when hand function is limited. The pots have heavy bottoms, which ensures that heat is transferred evenly and decreases the chance that the pot will slide around when you're stirring.

Most of the ordinary cooking utensils work in my kitchen, although I find those with a rubber grip are best for my needs. Visit your local shops and get a hands-on feel for what suits your particular kitchen and works best for your needs.

A WORD ABOUT SALT

In the 10 years since my injury I've had to adjust to a completely new life. After a spinal cord injury you discover that it's not just your mobility that is affected. In fact, much of what you took for granted, like what kind of food you eat, no longer applies.

I have had adverse reactions to some foods, which has forced me to change my diet. It has taken years of intently listening to my body to discover the cause of these reactions. The most noticeable reaction was an increase in spasticity and neurogenic pain as a result of consuming processed salts such as monosodium glutamate, better known as MSG. Even the slightest amount of MSG causes an incredible disturbance in how my body functions. Most noticeably, my spasticity is increased to an intensity and frequency that can only be described as dangerous. Occasionally during my discovery process I would experiment with this and the results included me flying out of my chair onto the floor. My body would be in such intense pain I would be unable to sleep for days.

But food requires seasoning to bring out its flavour! Even when I added table salt to my pasta water, the results would be the same—more pain and no sleep. It wasn't until I tried Himalayan pink salt in its pure form that I was able to season my food without terrible consequences. I can't overemphasize how this unrefined salt has brought the joy of cooking back into my life. For years I cooked and ate extremely bland food for fear of having a reaction, but the discovery of Himalayan pink salt has re-inspired me in the kitchen, and I can once again enjoy all the flavours of my food. And I feel great! It doesn't leave food tasting at all salty. In fact, it seems to bring out the flavours already present that might otherwise go unnoticed. The salt is so gentle it can even be used as bathing salt, and the reported cleansing effects of a 30-minute Himalayan pink salt bath can equal those of a three-day detox!

Himalayan pink salt is a distinctively pink, natural, mineral-rich luxury salt from the foothills of the Himalayan Mountains. It takes over 250 million years to form and comes from a time when the Earth was environmentally pure. It is thought

to be the highest-quality natural crystal salt available anywhere. It was once reserved exclusively for royalty and nicknamed "the King's salt" or "salt of life."

Unlike other salts, Himalayan pink salt contains all of the 84 trace minerals found in the human body and, remarkably, in the same proportions. Perhaps these similarities are why I don't have the negative reactions I do with other salts. Whatever the reason, it works for me and I'm very happy to have the flavour of well-seasoned food back in my life. I encourage you to try it for yourself, and even if you can't taste the difference you'll know that you're using a superior, healthier, higher-quality ingredient.

Many specialty food stores carry this type of high-grade salt. You can also purchase it directly through my friend Christyna Melnyk. Check out her website at www.saltoflife.ca.

APPETIZERS

Makes 20 boats
Prep time: 15 minutes
Cook time: none

ENDIVE BOATS WITH BLUE CHEESE

Have you ever been invited to a dinner party but had no idea what to bring? Well, here's an opportunity to put together a fantastic appetizer with very little effort and even less time. These little delights pack a wonderful crunchy punch, and the fact that they're in hand-held bites certainly makes them out of the ordinary. They are especially nice around the holiday season because of the festive colours.

CORY'S TIPS

» If any of your guests have nut allergies, simply omit the walnuts.
» Similarly, for those with lactose intolerance, you may substitute goat cheese for the blue cheese.
» For something a little out of the ordinary, substitute a specialty oil such as hazelnut, walnut, or even almond oil for the olive oil.

3 heads endive
7 oz (200 g) crumbled blue cheese
10 cherry tomatoes, halved
½ cup (125 mL) chopped toasted walnuts
2 Tbsp (30 mL) extra virgin olive oil
1 Tbsp (15 mL) balsamic vinegar
1 tsp (5 mL) freshly ground black pepper
1 tsp (5 mL) sea salt

Separate the endive leaves and arrange 20 on a serving dish. Divide the blue cheese and cherry tomatoes among the endive boats. Sprinkle with the toasted walnuts. In a small bowl, whisk the oil, vinegar, pepper, and salt until combined and drizzle over the endive boats. Enjoy!

Serves 4 to 6
Prep time: 15 minutes
Cook time: 35 minutes

BAKED VEGETABLE CRISPS WITH FIERY ALMOND DIP

This dish was on the menu at a sponsorship fundraiser I held. I had to have six friends help me prepare it, and it took a great deal of time because we were cooking for nearly 300 people! But in small batches it takes no time at all. And beware—the dip is highly addictive.

CORY'S TIPS
» A small deep fryer may be used instead of baking in the oven. Although this option is not as healthy as baking, it an acceptable substitute if you use unsaturated oils.
» A mandoline is almost a must in order to get really uniform slices.

VEGETABLE CRISPS
3 large purple potatoes
2 large yellow potatoes
2 large sweet potatoes
2 Tbsp (30 mL) olive oil

FIERY ALMOND DIP
2 tsp (10 mL) extra virgin olive oil
1 large shallot, finely chopped
2 cloves garlic, chopped
½ cup (125 mL) almond butter, at room temperature
1 Tbsp (15 mL) honey
1 tsp (5 mL) sea salt
1 tsp (5 mL) freshly ground black pepper
1 tsp (5 mL) ground cayenne
½ tsp (2 mL) ground cumin
½ tsp (2 mL) ground coriander
1 Tbsp (15 mL) lime juice

Preheat the oven to 425°F (220°C). Wash the potatoes well. Using a mandoline, food processor, or knife, slice all the potatoes as thinly as possible and place in a medium bowl. Add the olive oil and toss the slices until they are evenly coated with oil. Spread on a rimmed baking sheet. Bake for 35 minutes, turning frequently, until the slices are crisp and golden. Remove and cool on a rack.

To make the dip, combine the olive oil, shallot, and garlic in a medium saucepan over medium heat. Cook until softened, approximately 5 minutes. Stir in the almond butter, honey, salt, pepper, cayenne, cumin, and coriander. Remove from the heat and mix in the lime juice. If the dip is too thick, mix in a few tablespoons of hot water until the desired consistency is reached. Place in a serving bowl for dipping.

Serves 4 to 6
Prep time: 20 minutes
Cook time: none

MANGO & GOAT CHEESE WRAPS

When goat cheese is fresh, it is crumbly with a creamy texture, but it will become firmer as it ages. Goat cheese is rich in protein and contains potassium, vitamin A, thiamine, and niacin. It's actually lower in calories, fat, and cholesterol than cheddar or cream cheese, and some people find it easier to digest than cheese made from cow's milk.

CORY'S TIP

» If you are not partial to goat cheese, substitute cream cheese or your favourite variety of soft cheese.

8 oz (250 g) goat cheese
3 sprigs fresh basil, finely chopped
2 Tbsp (30 mL) extra virgin olive oil
1 tsp (5 mL) sea salt
1 tsp (5 mL) freshly ground black pepper
3 large ripe mangoes

Leave the goat cheese at room temperature for 30 to 40 minutes to soften. In a small bowl mix the cheese, basil, olive oil, salt, and pepper until well combined. Form the mixture into 25 small oval balls. Set aside.

With a potato peeler, peel and discard the mango skin, then peel off long strips of the flesh. Lay the mango strips flat on your work surface. Place a cheese ball at one end of a strip and roll it up. Insert a toothpick to hold it together. Repeat with the remaining ingredients, cover with plastic wrap, and refrigerate until serving time. These are best eaten the same day they are made.

Makes 12 stacks
Prep time: 10 minutes
Cook time: 5 minutes

ROASTED RED PEPPER & BRIE CRACKER STACKS

If you ever get that craving for a crunchy but creamy snack with a hint of spice and sweetness, look no further. This is a perfect example of balancing sweet, salty, spicy, and sour. I like to spice mine up a bit by adding a finely chopped cayenne chili pepper to the red pepper jelly. I don't think there's a simpler recipe for entertaining friends—or for a great late-night snack. The only problem is stopping yourself from eating them all!

12 low-sodium Triscuit crackers
7 oz (200 g) brie cheese
¼ cup (60 mL) roasted red pepper jelly

Preheat the oven to 400°F (200°C). Place the crackers on a large baking sheet. Cut the brie into small wedges, and place on the crackers. Top each with 1 tsp (5 mL) of the jelly. Bake for 5 minutes or until the cheese has softened. Serve immediately to your favourite friends!

CORY'S TIP
» Instead of brie, you can use Camembert or even Saint-André.

Makes 12 halves
Prep time: 10 minutes
Cook time: 10 minutes

THE DEVIL'S EGGS

Now here's a dish everyone will recognize. My father's free-run chickens lay eggs regularly, and my mother always served these at her dinner parties. I have continued the tradition but have added my own spicy twist—beautiful fresh red cayenne chilies (see tip), which I get from my garden. The colour is absolutely amazing, and I have yet to find anyone who doesn't enjoy these little appetizers.

CORY'S TIPS

» If you like it really hot, try adding one fresh red cayenne chili pepper (seeded and finely chopped).

» My use of Miracle Whip is a personal choice, as it adds a tangy zip, but regular mayonnaise may be substituted if you prefer.

6 eggs
1 Tbsp (15 mL) light Miracle Whip
¼ tsp (1 mL) Dijon mustard
1 tsp (5 mL) white balsamic vinegar
1 tsp (5 mL) ground cayenne
1 tsp (5 mL) madras curry powder
½ tsp (2 mL) sea salt
½ tsp (2 mL) freshly ground black pepper
¼ cup (60 mL) finely chopped chives

Place the eggs in a large saucepan and add enough cold water to completely cover them. Bring to a boil, then reduce the heat and simmer gently for 10 minutes. Remove from the heat. Drain and let cool.

When the eggs are cool, remove the shell and cut them lengthwise. Remove the yolks and place them in a medium bowl. Add the Miracle Whip, mustard, balsamic vinegar, cayenne chili, and curry powder to the yolks. Mash until well combined. Season with the salt and pepper. Gently mix in the chopped chives. Carefully spoon the mixture into the egg-white halves. Serve with a glass of water—and a fire extinguisher!

Serves 4
Prep time: 5 minutes
Cook time: 40 minutes

ROASTED GARLIC SPREAD

A number of years ago my house was for sale and I was cleaning windows, mopping floors, and dusting everywhere to make it attractive to buyers. But it wasn't good housekeeping that sold my house—it was the bulbs of garlic roasting in the oven midafternoon! Scores of people walking through the house commented on how wonderful it smelled. I sold my house thanks to this recipe!

CORY'S TIP

» I like to add a bit of honey to the top of each bulb for a little sweetness.

3 whole bulbs garlic
2 Tbsp (30 mL) olive oil
1 tsp (5 mL) sea salt
1 tsp (5 mL) freshly ground black pepper

Preheat the oven to 400°F (200°C). Carefully cut a ½ inch (1 cm) off the top of each garlic bulb and discard. Place the bulbs on a small rimmed baking sheet and drizzle with olive oil, thoroughly coating each bulb. Sprinkle with the salt and pepper. Cover with foil and bake in the centre of the oven for 30 to 40 minutes or until the cloves feel soft.

Allow the bulbs to cool, and squeeze the cloves out of their skins. Spread on your favourite crackers or toasted breads.

Makes about 30 mushroom caps
Prep time: 15 minutes
Cook time: 25 minutes

ITALIAN SAUSAGE—STUFFED MUSHROOM CAPS

This recipe came to me from my good friend Frederic. It is a simple appetizer, but the pairing of mushrooms and Italian sausage is wonderful. The last time I made them I substituted chorizo sausage and it was a great success. Next time I think I'll try fresh venison sausage, as I love wild game when I can get it.

CORY'S TIPS

» Try experimenting with other sausage, such as hot Italian or Thuringian.

» The stuffed caps can be made the night before and kept covered in the refrigerator until you're ready to finish them in the oven. Just be sure to let them come to room temperature before you bake them, as you want them to be heated thoroughly.

½ lb (250 g) button mushrooms (about 30)
½ lb (250 g) Italian sausage, casings removed
½ cup (125 mL) shredded mozzarella
¼ cup (60 mL) panko (Japanese breadcrumbs)
½ tsp (2 mL) freshly ground black pepper

Preheat the oven to 450°F (230°C). Remove the stems from the mushrooms and chop coarsely. Set the mushroom caps aside. In a large skillet over medium heat, cook the sausage and mushroom stems until cooked through, about 10 minutes. Remove from the heat and place on paper towels to drain.

In a large mixing bowl combine the sausage mixture, mozzarella, panko, and pepper. Spoon the mixture into the mushroom caps and place on a large, rimmed baking sheet. Bake for 15 minutes. Serve immediately.

Makes 12 figs
Prep time: 15 minutes
Cook time: 10 minutes

PROSCIUTTO-WRAPPED BALSAMIC FIGS STUFFED WITH GORGONZOLA

Figs with prosciutto and cheese might seem strange—but let me assure you that the combination will surprise and amaze you with its complexity. When I feel like a milder-flavoured cheese, I also enjoy this dish made with Cambozola instead of Gorgonzola (see Tip page 134).

CORY'S TIPS

» Use any soft, ripened cheese in place of the Gorgonzola.
» Keep your cheese in the refrigerator until you absolutely need it, as this will help keep it firm when cutting it.
» Medjool dates may be used in place of the figs, but be sure to remove the pits.

12 whole fresh figs, stems removed
7 oz (200 g) Gorgonzola, cubed
12 slices prosciutto
1 Tbsp (15 mL) balsamic vinegar
1 tsp (5 mL) sea salt
1 tsp (5 mL) freshly ground black pepper

Preheat the oven to 425°F (220°C). Cut an X in the figs three-quarters through, from top to bottom. Stuff a piece of cheese into the centre of each fig and wrap with one slice of prosciutto. Drizzle a little of the vinegar over each and season with the salt and pepper. Place on a rimmed baking sheet and bake for 8 to 10 minutes or until the cheese is melted.

Makes about 24 caps
Prep time: 10 minutes
Cook time: 20 minutes

ESCARGOTS IN CRIMINI MUSHROOM CAPS

This is another tribute to my mother, who made these for my birthday dinners. (You probably think that I was spoiled with all this wonderful food, but birthdays only come once a year!) These make an excellent party appetizer as well. You can even omit the mushrooms—simply bake the escargots in a shallow dish and serve with toothpicks. Add some garlic toast or an assortment of your favourite breads for a perfect feast.

CORY'S TIP

» If brown crimini mushrooms are not available, white button mushrooms will work just fine.

7 oz (200 g) can escargots (approx 24)
24 brown crimini mushrooms, stems removed
2 Tbsp (30 mL) butter
1 shallot, finely chopped
2 cloves garlic, finely chopped
1 tsp (5 mL) sea salt
1 tsp (5 mL) freshly ground black pepper

Preheat the oven to 350°F (180°C). Drain and rinse the escargots. Place the mushroom caps in a single layer on a large, rimmed baking sheet and stuff with the escargots.

Place a small saucepan over medium-high heat and add the butter, shallot, garlic, salt, and pepper. Cook the shallot and garlic until softened, about 5 minutes. Drizzle over the mushroom caps and bake in the oven for 15 to 20 minutes or until the mushroom caps are tender. Serve hot.

Serves 4 to 6
Prep time: 15 minutes
Cook time: 10 minutes

COCONUT-CHIPOTLE MUSSELS

This recipe is one of my all-time favourites. Countless people have told me they don't like mussels, but as soon as the wonderful aroma of this dish filled the kitchen, they were lined up. And when every last mussel had been consumed, the same people would beg for more. So serve this at your next dinner party and see how many people you can convert into mussel lovers. Perfect for alfresco dining, especially when accompanied by fresh, warm focaccia bread and a light Pinot Gris.

CORY'S TIPS

» If you want to substitute fresh clams for the mussels, be sure to soak them in salted water for a minimum of one hour to purge any sand they may have sucked up.
» For a more aromatic Thai flavour, add lemon grass to the shallot and garlic in the pot.
» Chipotle powder can be found in specialty markets or the import section of many grocery stores.
» If you do not have chipotle powder, canned chipotle chilies in adobo sauce work equally well but you will have to experiment to find the level of heat that suits you.

1 Tbsp (15 mL) olive oil
1 shallot, finely chopped
2 cloves garlic, finely chopped
1 Tbsp (15 mL) chipotle powder
14 oz (398 mL) can light coconut milk
2 lb (1 kg) fresh mussels

Place a large deep pot over medium-high heat and add the olive oil, shallot, and garlic. Cook until the shallot and garlic are softened, about 3 minutes. Add the chipotle powder and coconut milk, and continue cooking until reduced by one-third. Add the mussels and stir. Cover the pot and allow to steam until the mussels open, approximately 3 minutes. Discard any mussels that do not open. Pour into a serving bowl and serve with your favourite bread to mop up the juice.

Serves 4
Prep time: 10 minutes
Cook time: 20 minutes

CLAMS WITH FRESH FENNEL CREAM

This recipe is the result of an experiment. I have always known that the licorice flavour of fennel pairs very well with seafood, but had not tried fresh fennel seeds. The result was absolutely fantastic, as I'm sure you'll agree. Sometimes it takes a little bravery and willingness to think outside the box to create memorable and successful dishes. Occasionally you may be unsuccessful, but don't let that stop you. A recipe is simply a guideline; nothing is written in stone when it comes to your own creative culinary adventures.

CORY'S TIP

» Fresh fennel seeds are best, but the dried ones will work too. Just be sure to bruise them first with a mortar and pestle, or by pressing very hard with the side of your chef's knife, to release their aromatic oils.

1 Tbsp (15 mL) olive oil
1 shallot, finely chopped
2 cloves garlic, finely chopped
1 Tbsp (15 mL) fresh fennel seeds, lightly crushed
2 fresh red cayenne chilies, seeded and finely chopped
1 cup (250 mL) light cream
½ cup (125 mL) dry white wine
2 lb (1 kg) fresh, live clams, cleaned
¼ cup (60 mL) chopped fresh parsley

Place a large stockpot over medium-high heat and add the olive oil, shallots, and garlic. Cook until softened, about 5 minutes. Add the fennel seeds, chilies, cream, and wine, and bring to a boil. Reduce the heat to medium and cook for about 10 minutes.

Add the clams and parsley, and mix thoroughly. Cover and steam for 5 minutes or until the clams have opened. Discard any that do not open. Pour into a serving bowl and serve with warm focaccia for dipping.

Serves 8
Prep time: 10 minutes
Cook time: 10 minutes

CLAMS OREGANO ON SEASHELLS

This recipe has a funny story behind it. I didn't realize that barnacles have a tendency to explode when heated. When I accidentally made this dish with barnacle-covered seashells, my guests thought I was making popcorn in the oven! Some things you just have to find out the hard way, I guess. I should've taken a picture to show you the disaster I created. The explosions shot rock salt absolutely everywhere inside my oven! In the end the dish was a success, aside from having to clean up the mess. Check with your local seafood market to find clean, barnacle-free seashells.

CORY'S TIPS

» Don't be bothered if you cannot find shells that are clean and barnacle free—these clams taste fantastic in regular baking dishes.

» Rock salt may be purchased at your local grocery market.

½ cup (125 mL) butter, melted
1 cup (250 mL) panko (Japanese breadcrumbs)
2 cloves garlic, finely chopped
2 Tbsp (30 mL) finely chopped fresh parsley
3 Tbsp (45 mL) grated Parmesan cheese
1 Tbsp (15 mL) lemon juice
1 Tbsp (15 mL) chopped fresh oregano
¼ tsp (1 mL) red pepper flakes
Two 7 oz (200 g) cans clams, drained and
    chopped
2 cups (500 mL) rock salt
Lime wedges

Combine the butter, panko, garlic, parsley, Parmesan cheese, lemon juice, oregano, and red pepper flakes in a medium bowl. Add the chopped clams and mix thoroughly. Spoon the mixture into scallop shells, oyster shells, or small baking dishes.

Preheat the broiler. Cover the bottom of a rimmed baking sheet with a ½-inch-deep (1 cm) layer of rock salt. Sprinkle with a little water to dampen. Arrange the filled shells on the rock salt and place under the broiler until golden brown, about 10 minutes. Serve hot, garnished with the lime wedges.

Makes 12 cakes
Prep time: 20 minutes
Cook time: 10 minutes

CORY'S CRISPY CRUNCHY CRAB CAKES

When the opportunity arises and I am able to purchase fresh crab locally, I can't help but make these crunchy delights for my friends. Working with fresh live crabs can be rather dangerous; I have experienced an uncomfortable pinch from time to time. Whenever possible I have my fishmonger or a hungry friend give me a hand cleaning and cooking them.

CORY'S TIPS

» Take care not to burn the panko breading.
» Serve immediately, otherwise the panko crust will become soggy.

2 cups (500 mL) cooked crabmeat (about 2 crabs)
2 eggs, lightly beaten
4 shallots, finely chopped
1 fresh red cayenne chili, seeded and finely chopped
1 tsp (5 mL) chopped capers
½ cup (125 mL) finely chopped fresh parsley
½ cup (125 mL) finely chopped cilantro with stalks
1 tsp (5 mL) lime zest
2 Tbsp (30 mL) lime juice
1 tsp (5 mL) sea salt
½ tsp (2 mL) freshly ground black pepper
2 cups (500 mL) panko (Japanese breadcrumbs)
2 Tbsp (30 mL) olive oil
Lime wedges (optional)
Chili-Lime Mayo (page 37)

In a large mixing bowl, gently combine the crabmeat, eggs, shallots, chili, capers, parsley, cilantro, lime zest and juice, salt, pepper, and 1 cup (250 mL) of the panko. Using an ice cream scoop or large spoon, scoop about ¼ cup (60 mL) of the mixture into your hands and gently roll it into a ball. Use a fork to press the ball into a patty. Repeat with the remaining mixture. Press the remaining 1 cup (250 mL) panko evenly onto both sides of the patties.

Place a large skillet on medium-high heat and add the olive oil. Cook the crab cakes for 2 to 3 minutes per side until they are cooked through and lightly browned on both sides. Serve hot, garnished with lime wedges (if using), and drizzle with Chili-Lime Mayo.

Makes 12 prawns
Prep time: 30 minutes
Cook time: 15 minutes

CHIPOTLE & LIME PROSCIUTTO-WRAPPED PRAWNS

I recently made this dish for a fundraiser dinner to help promote this very cookbook, and it was a success. I really wanted to showcase my skills and creativity in the kitchen, and this appetizer speaks loud and clear. It may sound simple, and it is, but my guests went absolutely crazy over it, and I'm sure yours will, too. Quite often the foods we consume are overprocessed and their natural sweetness and flavour become lost. "Less is more" holds true in this recipe; it allows the wonderful flavours to come together, pure and simple.

CORY'S TIP

» Hot paprika or dried chilies can be used instead of chipotle powder. If you like heat, simply add more powder!

1 Tbsp (15 mL) lime zest
2 Tbsp (30 mL) lime juice
2 Tbsp (30 mL) extra virgin olive oil
¼ tsp (1 mL) chipotle powder
12 large prawns, shelled and deveined
6 strips prosciutto, cut in half

In a small mixing bowl combine the lime zest, lime juice, olive oil, and chipotle powder until thoroughly incorporated. Place the prawns in the mixture and stir gently to make sure each piece is well coated. Cover and refrigerate for 30 minutes.

Preheat the oven to 450°F (230°C). Working with one at a time, wrap a half piece of prosciutto around each prawn and place on a large rimmed baking sheet. Brush the remaining lime-chipotle mixture on the outside of the prosciutto-wrapped prawns. Bake in the centre of the oven for 10 to 12 minutes or until the prawns are pink and the prosciutto is crisp.

Makes 12 prawns
Prep time: 20 minutes
Cook time: 20 minutes

CORY'S FAMOUS FRAZZLED PRAWNS & WASABI MAYO

If I had to pick my favourite appetizer recipe, this would have to be it. The first time I made these, I soaked the bamboo skewers in cold water to keep them from burning like they do on the barbecue. Not a good idea! Water and hot oil do not mix, which I found out the hard way, when my pot overflowed everywhere. Use the largest prawns you can find for this recipe, or even rock lobster if it's available. Just talking about it makes my mouth water, and I think I will make them tonight. (I didn't make these famous, they made *me* famous!) You will need 12 skewers to make this, one for each prawn.

CORY'S TIPS

» Kataifi phyllo dough is sold at most Mediterranean and import delicatessens, although four sheets of regular phyllo pastry, air dried on a cooling rack and chopped fine, can be substituted.

» I recommend using large prawns, but if you're stuck with a smaller size just adjust your cooking time.

1 cup (250 mL) panko (Japanese breadcrumbs)
1 cup (250 mL) dried and finely chopped kataifi phyllo pastry
1 tsp (5 mL) sea salt
1 tsp (5 mL) freshly ground black pepper
½ cup (125 mL) rice flour
1 egg, lightly beaten
4 cups (1 L) vegetable or peanut oil
12 large prawns, shelled and deveined
½ cup (125 mL) light mayonnaise
1 Tbsp (15 mL) wasabi

On a shallow plate, mix the panko and phyllo, and season with salt and pepper. Place the rice flour and beaten egg on two separate shallow plates. Skewer each prawn lengthwise on a skewer and dredge in the rice flour. Shake off the excess and coat in the egg. Coat with the panko-phyllo mixture and set aside.

Place the oil in a deep medium saucepan over medium-high heat. The best way to tell when the oil is hot enough is to use a thermometer; it should be at 365°F (185°C). But you can also drop a small piece of potato in the oil and when it floats, you're ready to start cooking! Carefully add the skewered prawns, four at a time, and cook until golden brown, about 4 minutes. Drain on paper towels. Repeat with the remaining skewers.

In a small bowl, combine the mayonnaise and wasabi. Serve the skewers with the dip.

Makes 20 prawns
Prep time: 20 minutes
Cook time: 10 minutes

CHILI PRAWNS WITH GARLIC AIOLI

Living on an island offers me the opportunity to enjoy the freshest seafood available. Nowadays the fishing and seafood industry uses state-of-the-art technology to deliver freshly caught seafood flash-frozen at sea, so don't let "previously frozen" deter you, because its quality is comparable to fresh. My heart goes out to people with a seafood allergy who don't get to enjoy dishes like this. Sorry, Deni!

PRAWNS

1 fresh red cayenne chili, seeded and finely chopped
½ tsp (2 mL) hot paprika
½ tsp (2 mL) ground coriander
2 cloves garlic, finely chopped
2 Tbsp (30 mL) lime juice
2 Tbsp (30 mL) olive oil
½ tsp (2 mL) sea salt
½ tsp (2 mL) freshly ground black pepper
20 large prawns, shelled and deveined

GARLIC AIOLI

1½ cups (375 mL) light mayonnaise
2 cloves garlic, finely chopped
1 tsp (5 mL) Dijon or grainy mustard

Preheat the barbecue to 375°F (190°C). In a large mixing bowl, combine the cayenne chili, paprika, coriander, garlic, lime juice, olive oil, salt, and pepper. Mix thoroughly. Add the prawns, mix well, cover, and refrigerate for 30 minutes. While the prawns are marinating, soak 20 bamboo skewers in water.

Thread each prawn on a soaked bamboo skewer and barbecue until pink, approximately 2 minutes per side.

To make the aioli, combine the mayonnaise, garlic, and mustard in a small bowl, and serve with the prawns for dipping.

Serves 4
Prep time: 25 minutes
Cook time: 5 minutes

CRUNCHY SQUID WITH CHILI-LIME MAYO

This is a take on the traditional calamari that you may have eaten at your favourite restaurant. As you will see with this recipe, dining at home can be fun and even more flavourful than at a restaurant. If you have a portable hot plate, take it outside so you won't cause your home to smell like hot oil. The fresh chilies make all the difference, especially if you can get them from your garden like I do.

CORY'S TIPS

» When shopping for squid, look in the frozen foods section, where they are readily available—and they're already cleaned.

» Rice flour may be substituted for the wheat flour for those with wheat allergies.

CHILI-LIME MAYO

5 Tbsp (75 mL) light mayonnaise
2 fresh red cayenne chilies, seeded and finely chopped
1 Tbsp (15 mL) lemon zest
1 Tbsp (15 mL) lime zest
2 Tbsp (30 mL) lemon juice
2 Tbsp (30 mL) lime juice

CRUNCHY SQUID

2 cups (500 mL) vegetable or peanut oil
2 cups (500 mL) all-purpose flour
1 lb (500 g) squid, cleaned, scored, and tentacles removed
1 tsp (5 mL) sea salt
1 tsp (5 mL) freshly ground black pepper
Lemon wedges

To make the Chili-Lime Mayo, combine the mayonnaise, chilies, lemon zest, lime zest, lemon juice, and lime juice in a medium bowl and mix thoroughly. Refrigerate while you cook the squid.

Place a large deep stockpot over medium-high heat and add the oil. Bring the temperature to 350°F (180°C). (If you do not have a thermometer, carefully place a small piece of potato in the oil; when the potato floats to the surface, the oil is the right temperature.) Pour the flour onto a large serving plate. Toss the squid in the flour and shake off any excess. Carefully place in the oil. When the squid is crispy and golden, after 3 to 5 minutes, remove with tongs and place on paper towels to drain. Season with the salt and pepper while hot.

Serve the hot squid with the mayo dip and garnish with lemon wedges on the side.

Serves 4
Prep time: 15 minutes
Cook time: 25 minutes

BAKED SEA SCALLOPS IN PANKO CRUST

I first had this dish while travelling in Europe a number of years ago. It was my twentieth birthday and I treated myself to a night out in Belgium. What a night! You are going to absolutely love this recipe, as it takes no time at all and is a fantastic appetizer or main course. It looks wonderful on the plate and tastes even better. Be sure to make a few extras, as your guests will finish every last one! Whenever you are cooking with wine, buy a good-quality bottle, as you never want to use wine you wouldn't drink. Life is too short to drink bad wine!

CORY'S TIP
» The best scallops for this dish are Digby or large swimming scallops since they tend to be larger than other scallops.

2 lb (1 kg) fresh scallops
1 cup (250 mL) white wine
1 tsp (5 mL) sea salt
4 Tbsp (60 mL) butter
1 shallot, finely chopped
2 Tbsp (30 mL) all-purpose flour
1 cup (250 mL) panko (Japanese breadcrumbs)

Preheat the oven to 400°F (200°C). Place a medium saucepan over medium-high heat and add the scallops, wine, and salt. Bring to a boil, reduce the heat to a simmer, and cook for an additional 4 minutes. Remove the scallops to a rimmed baking dish big enough to fit the scallops in a single layer. Reserve the cooking liquid to use later.

Place the same saucepan over medium-high heat and melt 2 Tbsp (30 mL) of the butter. Add the shallot and cook until softened, about 5 minutes. Sprinkle the flour over the butter and shallot, and whisk it in. Pour in the reserved cooking liquid, whisking continuously. When the sauce has thickened, after about 5 minutes, pour it over the scallops in the baking dish. Stir thoroughly. Sprinkle the panko overtop and dot with the remaining 2 Tbsp (30 mL) butter. Bake for 15 minutes or until bubbly and brown. Serve these appetizers with fondue forks or toothpicks.

Makes 6 scallops
Prep time: 15 minutes
Cook time: 6 minutes

PROSCIUTTO-WRAPPED SEA SCALLOPS WITH CHILI MAYO

When I was young my mother would make scallops wrapped in bacon as a special birthday dinner, so this is a recipe I never grow tired of. It's also been responsible for consistently getting me second dates. It's simple, but the flavours of prosciutto and sea scallops are a match made in heaven. Use the largest scallops you can find, as the meaty texture makes all the difference. The prosciutto is very high in sodium so additional salt is not needed.

CORY'S TIP

» You can substitute any chili sauce of your choosing for the sambal oelek, depending on how hot you like it. Sambal oelek is very hot, and you'll need to experiment with a level of heat that suits you. Most grocers will carry it in their import section, along with many other varieties of hot sauce.

6 large sea scallops
6 slices prosciutto
1 Tbsp (15 mL) olive oil
1 Tbsp (15 mL) butter
1 tsp (5 mL) freshly ground black pepper
¼ cup (60 mL) light mayonnaise
1 Tbsp (15 mL) sambal oelek
Lime wedges

Dry the scallops using paper towels, and wrap each in one slice of prosciutto. In a large saucepan, heat the olive oil and butter on medium-high heat. Add the wrapped scallops and sprinkle with the pepper. Cook for 3 minutes on each side or until golden brown.

In a small mixing bowl, combine the mayonnaise with the sambal chili sauce. Serve the hot scallops with the dipping sauce and garnish with lime wedges.

Serves 4
Prep time: 10 minutes
Cook time: 5 minutes

BLACK & BLUE TUNA SUSHI WITH CHILI-LIME MAYO

This recipe is definitely a winner with sushi lovers, and it may just convert you if you're not one already. Your local fishmonger should be able to provide you with sushi-grade ahi tuna, but if you are unsuccessful, try asking at your local sushi restaurant. My favourite sushi restaurant introduced me to this dish, for which I am forever grateful. Thank you, Eric and Larry!

CORY'S TIPS

» If black sesame seeds are unavailable, you can lightly toast the white ones for a contrast in colour.

» Sometimes I sear the tuna with chili oil for an added flavour kick.

2 Tbsp (30 mL) black sesame seeds
2 Tbsp (30 mL) white sesame seeds
4 blocks (each 3 oz/90 g) ahi tuna, sushi grade
1 tsp (5 mL) sea salt
1 tsp (5 mL) freshly ground black pepper
1 Tbsp (15 mL) olive oil
Lime wedges
Chili-Lime Mayo (page 37)

Place the black sesame seeds on one shallow plate and the white sesame seeds on another. Working with one block at a time, press the tuna blocks into the seeds, alternating black and white seeds on opposite sides of the block. Season with salt and pepper.

Place a large saucepan over medium-high heat and add the olive oil. When the oil is hot, add the coated tuna blocks, rotating them to cook on each side for 1 minute. Remove and slice on the bias into bite-sized pieces. Serve with lime wedges and the mayo for dipping.

Makes 12 pockets
Prep time: 10 minutes
Cook time: 25 minutes

WEST COAST TOFU SALMON POCKET

This fantastic recipe will have people asking you, "What is this?" and "Where did you get the recipe?" The truth is I have enjoyed this recipe at a number of different restaurants. The flavour combination works perfectly and I especially like that these little pockets can be hand-held—*and* they are actually pretty good for you! Anyone who enjoys sushi will absolutely love them. And if someone does not enjoy sushi or this version of it, then there's just more for everyone else.

CORY'S TIPS

» Abura-age is tofu that is thinly sliced and deep-fried, which makes it puff up and form a pouch. Look for it in most Asian and import markets.

» If you can't find tobiko, try lumpfish roe instead. Check with your local fishmonger or sushi shop for ordering details.

1½ cups (375 mL) water
1 cup (250 mL) short-grain white rice
1 Tbsp (15 mL) rice vinegar
3 Tbsp (45 mL) soy sauce
1 tsp (5 mL) honey
½ tsp (2 mL) wasabi
12 abura-age pockets (deep-fried tofu; see
    Tips below)
1 avocado, pitted, peeled, and sliced
10 oz (300 g) lox
3 Tbsp (45 mL) tobiko (flying fish roe)
2 tsp (10 mL) toasted black sesame seeds

Place a medium saucepan over high heat, add the water, rice, and rice vinegar, and bring to a boil. Cover, reduce to a simmer, and cook for 20 minutes. Remove from the heat and let cool with the lid on the pot.

In a small mixing bowl, combine the soy sauce, honey, and wasabi, and set aside. Slit the abura-age open on one side to form a pocket. Roll the rice into 12 small logs; each should be able to fit into one pocket. Spoon about a teaspoon (5 mL) of the soy sauce mixture over each rice log. Top with a slice of avocado. Wrap each rice log with some lox and stuff into a pocket. Garnish each with a little tobiko and a sprinkle of the toasted black sesame seeds.

SOUPS & SALADS

Serves 4
Prep time: 15 minutes
Cook time: 10 minutes

SPINACH SALAD WITH POMEGRANATE-MOLASSES DRESSING

Sometimes even the best salads can seem a bit boring, but with this dressing, you can't go wrong. Even the kids will eat their greens! When the mood strikes me, I make a large batch of dressing and keep it in a squeeze bottle so it's ready to go whenever I am. I have even been guilty of bringing this dressing with me to a restaurant—it's that good.

CORY'S TIPS

» Look for pomegranate molasses at your local imported food market. If you are unable to find it, any fruit syrup can be substituted.
» I've enjoyed this salad with roasted almond oil instead of the standard olive oil.
» Cook your eggs ahead of time so they will be cool and ready to slice.
» The Parmesan crisps will burn very easily; be sure to watch them closely.

½ cup (125 mL) grated Parmesan cheese
4 cups (1 L) fresh spinach, large stems removed
¼ cup (60 mL) finely sliced red onion
½ cup (125 mL) sliced fresh mushrooms
2 eggs, hard-boiled and sliced
¼ cup (60 mL) dried cherries or cranberries (optional)
¼ cup (60 mL) toasted walnuts
5 oz (150 g) crumbled goat cheese (optional)
2 Tbsp (30 mL) pomegranate molasses (see Tip)
½ cup (125 mL) extra virgin olive oil
¼ cup (60 mL) red wine vinegar
2 Tbsp (30 mL) Dijon mustard

Preheat the oven to 400°F (200°C). Divide the Parmesan cheese into four even mounds on a silicone baking mat or non-stick baking sheet, and bake until melted and bubbly, about 10 minutes. Allow to cool for about 5 minutes while you assemble the salads.

In a large mixing bowl, combine the spinach leaves, onion, and mushrooms. Using tongs, portion the salad mixture into individual bowls and top with the egg slices, cherries or cranberries (if using), and walnuts. Sprinkle the goat cheese over the salads (if using). Whisk the pomegranate molasses, olive oil, red wine vinegar, and Dijon mustard in a small bowl until thoroughly combined. Pour over the salads. Garnish each with a Parmesan crisp.

Serves 4
Prep time: 10 minutes
Cook time: none

FENNEL-APPLE SALAD

If you've never tried fennel, you are truly missing out. I encourage everyone to experiment with this wonderful vegetable for its sweet flavour and exciting possibilities. It grows very quickly. A small section of my garden is dedicated to fennel plants. Nearby is an organic apple orchard, and since apples and fennel are ready to eat at the same time of year—late summer—you may guess that if you are at my house you'll be having this salad! It keeps very well when covered in the refrigerator and makes a great late-night snack.

CORY'S TIP

» When preparing fennel bulbs, keep the green fronds—they make a lovely garnish.

1 ripe apple, cored and thinly sliced
2 Tbsp (30 mL) lime juice
1 Tbsp (15 mL) lime zest
2 bulbs fennel, thinly sliced
½ cup (125 mL) dried cherries
1 tsp (5 mL) chopped fresh red cayenne chili (or to taste)
1 tsp (5 mL) sea salt
1 tsp (5 mL) freshly ground black pepper
1 Tbsp (15 mL) rice vinegar
¼ cup (60 mL) crumbled blue cheese (optional)
2 Tbsp (30 mL) toasted pistachios

In a large mixing bowl, toss the apple slices with the lime juice to prevent browning. Add the lime zest, fennel, cherries, chili, salt, pepper, and rice vinegar. Toss and divide among four serving bowls. Top with the blue cheese (if using) and pistachios. Enjoy!

Serves 4
Prep time: 10 minutes
Cook time: none

STRAWBERRY SPINACH SALAD

The first time I made this salad, it was a beautiful summer evening and friends had just stopped by. I grabbed my garden scissors, a bowl, and the rest of my ingredients, and made this salad right there in the garden for us to enjoy. I just love the sustainability of growing my own food, and nothing you can buy in a store can compare for flavour. My guests were impressed and have stopped by more than once in hopes of a repeat patio-dinner evening. Be sure to serve this one to people you like, as you'll probably be seeing more of them!

CORY'S TIPS

» If your guests have a nut allergy, substitute drained capers for the almonds.

» You can use any combination of salad greens that includes spinach.

6 cups (1.5 L) fresh spinach
2 cups (500 mL) stemmed and halved fresh strawberries
¼ cup (60 mL) extra virgin olive oil
2 Tbsp (30 mL) red wine vinegar
1½ tsp (7.5 mL) chopped fresh dill
1 Tbsp (15 mL) finely chopped shallots
1 clove garlic, finely chopped
1 Tbsp (15 mL) Dijon mustard
½ cup (125 mL) toasted unsalted almonds

Place the spinach in a large bowl and top with the strawberries. In a small bowl, thoroughly whisk together the olive oil, red wine vinegar, dill, shallots, garlic, and mustard. Pour the dressing over the salad and toss gently. Sprinkle with the toasted almonds and serve with a chilled Chardonnay. Enjoy!

Serves 4
Prep time: 10 minutes
Cook time: none

FRESH TOMATO, BASIL, & BOCCONCINI SALAD

The words *simple* and *fantastic* have never been better used than to describe this fresh little salad. This is probably the most traditional combination of flavours in my cookbook and for good reason. Everyone has to eat, and this salad makes it a very enjoyable experience. Use the best balsamic vinegar you can find, as it really does make a noticeable difference.

CORY'S TIPS

» You can purchase bocconcini the size of pearls or as small balls, and both work well in this recipe.
» I have substituted goat cheese for bocconcini for guests who are lactose intolerant.
» For a unique twist, try walnut, hazelnut, or even almond oil instead of the standard olive oil.

10 cherry tomatoes, halved
1 cup (250 mL) small bocconcini balls, drained and halved
1 cup (250 mL) finely chopped fresh basil
1 tsp (5 mL) sea salt
½ tsp (2 mL) freshly ground black pepper
2 Tbsp (30 mL) extra virgin olive oil
1 Tbsp (15 mL) balsamic vinegar

Divide the tomatoes and bocconcini among four serving plates. Sprinkle with the chopped fresh basil and season with the salt and pepper. Drizzle with the olive oil and balsamic vinegar. Serve as a fresh summer salad.

Serves 6
Prep time: 10 minutes
Cook time: 5 minutes

CRISPY PROSCIUTTO & ARTICHOKE SALAD

I have been growing artichoke plants for ten years and have yet to produce an artichoke that I can actually eat. I've surrendered to the fact that I have to buy artichokes because the plant in my garden only produces a beautiful flower. It looks very much like a thistle, but is absolutely stunning. If you can grow an edible version, artichoke is worth the small space it takes in the garden. I wish I could grow prosciutto, too!

CORY'S TIPS

» For an extra bit of flavour, use the artichoke oil instead of olive oil in your dressing.

» If you're not a fan of goat cheese, substitute some crumbled cow's feta or even grated Asiago for it.

10 oz (300 g) jar artichoke hearts in oil
10 slices prosciutto, cut in quarters
6 cups (1.5 L) spring salad mix
5 oz (150 g) crumbled goat cheese
2 Tbsp (30 mL) red wine vinegar
1 Tbsp (15 mL) honey
2 tsp (10 mL) Dijon mustard
½ tsp (2 mL) sea salt
½ tsp (2 mL) freshly ground black pepper
¼ cup (60 mL) extra virgin olive oil

Drain the artichokes and slice into bite-sized pieces. Place a large skillet over medium-high heat, add the prosciutto pieces, and cook until crisp, about 5 minutes. Remove to paper towels to drain any excess oil.

Evenly divide the salad mix among six salad plates and top with the prosciutto, artichokes, and crumbled goat cheese. To make the dressing, combine the vinegar, honey, mustard, salt, and pepper in a medium bowl and whisk until well incorporated. Gradually whisk in the olive oil until smooth. Drizzle the dressing over the salad and enjoy!

Serves 4
Prep time: 10 minutes
Cook time: none

PACIFIC SMOKED SALMON & APPLE SALAD

If you ever really want to impress your guests without having to do too much work, try this recipe and then sit back and enjoy the compliments. The fact that I have an organic apple orchard in my backyard encourages me to be creative with this basic fruit. This delicious salad makes an excellent starter to your dinner or accompaniment to a fantastic brunch—I like to serve it with a crisp white wine. Cold-smoked salmon works the best, although hot-smoked adds a unique texture to this salad.

CORY'S TIPS

» To create a thicker dressing, line a strainer with cheesecloth and drain 1 cup (250 mL) yogurt over a bowl in the refrigerator for about an hour. Then measure out ½ cup (125 mL) and add it to your dressing.

» If your smoked fish is high in sodium, reduce the amount of salt you add to the dish.

2 crisp red apples
3 Tbsp (45 mL) lime juice
2 cups (500 mL) arugula
½ lb (250 g) smoked salmon fillet
½ cup (125 mL) low-fat yogurt
1 Tbsp (15 mL) prepared horseradish
½ tsp (2 mL) sea salt
½ tsp (2 mL) freshly ground black pepper
1 Tbsp (15 mL) finely chopped chives

Thinly slice the apples, leaving the peel on, and remove the core. Toss the apple slices in a small mixing bowl with 2 Tbsp (30 mL) of the lime juice to prevent browning. Arrange the arugula on four serving plates. Remove the skin and any bones from the smoked salmon. Cut the salmon into thin strips at an angle. Arrange the salmon and apple slices on the arugula.

To make the dressing, combine the yogurt, remaining 1 Tbsp (15 mL) of lime juice, horseradish, salt, and pepper in a medium bowl, and stir until smooth. Drizzle over the salmon, apples, and arugula. Garnish with the chives.

Serves 8
Prep time: 10 minutes
Cook time: 5 minutes

EDAMAME SALAD WITH DAIKON & TOBIKO

Even those who shudder to think of eating tofu will come to love this healthy salad. Edamame, or green soybeans, are very high in protein and fibre, making this an excellent choice for vegetarians. Edamame grows extremely well in organic soils and has beautiful little flowers. A few of my friends are vegetarians, and their visits give me a great opportunity to make this salad (minus the tobiko, of course). But you don't need a vegetarian as a reason to make this salad!

CORY'S TIPS
» If you like your dressing a little sweeter, use mandarins canned in syrup.
» Edamame can be purchased in the frozen section, already shelled, if fresh is unavailable.

8 cups (2 L) water
2 tsp (10 mL) sea salt
2 lb (1 kg) shelled fresh edamame beans
10 oz (284 mL) can unsweetened mandarin segments
2 Tbsp (30 mL) rice vinegar
½ tsp (2 mL) freshly ground black pepper
1 shallot, finely chopped
1 Tbsp (15 mL) lime zest
2 Tbsp (30 mL) lime juice
1 daikon (Japanese radish), peeled and shredded
¼ cup (60 mL) tobiko (flying fish roe)

Place the water and 1 tsp (5 mL) of the salt in a large stockpot over medium-high heat and bring to a boil. Add the edamame and cook until fork tender, about 5 minutes.

While the edamame is cooking, combine the mandarins (including the juice), rice vinegar, pepper, shallot, and lime zest and juice in a small bowl, and mix thoroughly.

Drain the edamame and allow to cool. Spoon the cooled edamame evenly into eight serving bowls. Top each with the shredded daikon. Drizzle the dressing overtop. Sprinkle with the remaining 1 tsp (5 mL) salt and top with the tobiko.

Serves 6
Prep time: 10 minutes
Cook time: none

SHRIMP, CUCUMBER, & WATERMELON SALAD

This recipe comes to me by way of my neighbour Erin. I had never tried anything like this, nor would I have thought that the combination would be successful, but talk about a fresh, crisp, delicious blend of flavours! It will be unlike anything you've ever had before, but you'll want to have it on every warm summer evening. Thanks, Erin!

CORY'S TIP

» If you do not have Galliano, a little Pernod or white rum will work very well. The use of Angostura bitters is paramount; without it, this salad just doesn't have the bite it deserves.

3 lb (1.5 kg) watermelon, seeded and chopped in 1-inch cubes
½ lb (250 g) cooked baby shrimp
1 large cucumber, peeled and chopped in 1-inch cubes
1 fresh red cayenne chili, seeded and finely chopped
1 shallot, finely chopped
2 Tbsp (30 mL) roughly chopped fresh mint
2 Tbsp (30 mL) finely chopped fresh coriander leaves
2 Tbsp (30 mL) honey
1 Tbsp (15 mL) lime zest
2 Tbsp (30 mL) lime juice
1 Tbsp (15 mL) Galliano liqueur
¼ tsp (1 mL) Angostura bitters

Combine the watermelon, shrimp, cucumber, chili, shallot, mint, and coriander in a medium bowl, and toss to mix well. Evenly divide the mixture among six serving plates.

Stir the honey, lime zest, lime juice, Galliano, and Angostura bitters together in a small bowl until well incorporated. Lightly drizzle over the salads, cover with plastic wrap, and refrigerate until chilled.

Serves 4
Prep time: 10 minutes
Cook time: none

CRAB SALAD WITH PEARS & ROASTED PECANS

A friend emailed me from a fancy restaurant to say that he was enjoying the best salad he'd ever had in his whole life. I wasn't surprised when he told me what was in it. I've re-created the dish based on his description. This just may be the best salad *you*'ll ever have!

CORY'S TIPS

» I have also enjoyed this with canned albacore tuna instead of crabmeat.
» For an exciting twist, you can substitute Cory's Kickin' Cayenne Cocoa-Coated Pecans (page 162) for the roasted pecans.

½ cup (125 mL) finely chopped celery
¼ cup (60 mL) chopped roasted pecans
2 pears, finely chopped
¼ cup (60 mL) finely chopped red onion
2 Tbsp (30 mL) finely chopped fresh parsley
2 Tbsp (30 mL) lemon juice
1 Tbsp (15 mL) extra virgin olive oil
1 tsp (5 mL) freshly ground black pepper
¼ tsp (1 mL) sea salt
Two 4 oz (120 g) cans crabmeat or 8 oz (250 g) cooked fresh crabmeat
4 large butter lettuce leaves, rinsed and patted dry

Combine the celery, pecans, pears, onion, parsley, lemon juice, olive oil, pepper, and salt in a medium bowl. Gently fold in the crabmeat, being careful to not overmix. Place a lettuce leaf on each serving plate and portion the crab mixture on top. Enjoy this elegant salad with a sparkling wine.

Serves 4
Prep time: 10 minutes
Cook time: 10 minutes

BARBECUED TENDERLOIN STEAK SALAD WITH GOAT CHEESE

Now this is a salad that even men can get excited about! A barbecued steak can be paired with just about anything, and in this salad, it's absolute perfection. I had a wonderful time preparing this dish for a cooking video episode, and my video crew had an even better time eating the whole production! Be sure to heat your barbecue to very hot, as you really want to sear in the juices to keep the steak tender. My favourite cut of steak is the tenderloin, although any tender cut will do.

CORY'S TIPS

» If you don't have dried cranberries, any dried fruit can be substituted.
» My guests who are lactose intolerant can enjoy this one; I just substitute goat cheese for cow's feta.
» You can use any type or combination of greens, but the spiciness of arugula really stands up to the strong flavour of beef.

Two 6 oz (175 g) tenderloin steaks, thick cut
    (approx 2 inches/5 cm)
3 cups (750 mL) mixed baby greens
1 cup (250 mL) arugula
½ cup (125 mL) chopped toasted walnuts
½ red bell pepper, finely chopped
2 shallots, finely chopped
½ cup (125 mL) dried cranberries
4 oz (125 g) crumbled goat cheese
1 Tbsp (15 mL) extra virgin olive oil
2 tsp (10 mL) lemon juice
2 tsp (10 mL) white balsamic vinegar

Preheat the barbecue to 400°F (200°C). Cook the steaks to the desired doneness, about 2 minutes per side for medium-rare. Remove from the heat, tent loosely with foil, and allow to rest for 5 minutes.

Toss the mixed greens, arugula, walnuts, bell pepper, and shallots in a large salad bowl. Sprinkle with the cranberries and crumbled goat cheese. Combine the olive oil, lemon juice, and vinegar in a small bowl, and whisk until well incorporated.

Slice the steaks across the grain and arrange over the salad. Drizzle with the dressing and enjoy out on the patio.

Serves 4
Prep time: 10 minutes
Cook time: 25 minutes

HONEY-BALSAMIC CHICKEN SALAD

This recipe pays homage to my friend Bruno, who is also a chef. It has a unique blend of flavours and yet is so simple that every ingredient is identifiable. It remains my "foolproof" salad without being boring in the least. Thanks again, Bruno!

CORY'S TIP
» Serve this salad when the chicken is still hot; it makes a great contrast to the cold, crisp lettuce.

½ loaf focaccia bread, cut in 1-inch (2.5 cm) cubes
1 Tbsp (15 mL) olive oil
2 cloves garlic, finely chopped
1 shallot, finely chopped
12 oz (375 g) thinly sliced boneless, skinless chicken breast (approx 4 breasts)
½ tsp (2 mL) sea salt
½ tsp (2 mL) freshly ground black pepper
2 Tbsp (30 mL) honey
1 Tbsp (15 mL) balsamic vinegar
2 romaine hearts, roughly chopped
2 Tbsp (30 mL) grated Parmesan cheese

Preheat the oven to 375°F (190°C). Place the focaccia cubes on a large, rimmed baking sheet and bake in the centre of the oven until toasted, 10 to 15 minutes. Remove and set aside to cool.

Place a large saucepan over medium-high heat and add the oil, garlic, and shallot. Cook until softened, about 5 minutes, stirring frequently. Add the chicken, salt, and pepper. Cook until lightly browned on all sides, about 10 minutes. Whisk the honey and the balsamic vinegar together in a small bowl, add to the pan, and continue cooking for about 10 minutes.

Divide the lettuce among four serving bowls and top with the chicken and toasted focaccia. Sprinkle with the Parmesan cheese.

Serves 4
Prep time: 15 minutes
Cook time: 15 minutes

GARDEN-FRESH SPICY COUSCOUS SALAD

If you have 15 minutes to spare, you can make this fantastic, fresh-tasting dish. There are many variations on couscous salad, so don't hesitate to put your own twist on this dish to make it yours.

CORY'S TIPS

» I have found quinoa is a great alternative to couscous.

» For a little extra colour in your dish, use tri-colour couscous.

» You can toast pine nuts in a skillet over low heat. It will enhance their flavour wonderfully, but use extreme caution, as they burn very easily; be sure to stir them frequently and remove them from the heat promptly when they are lightly browned.

» Toasted pistachio nuts are an excellent alternative here.

3 Tbsp (45 mL) extra virgin olive oil
2 cloves garlic, finely chopped
1 shallot, finely chopped
1 tsp (5 mL) ground cumin
1½ cups (375 mL) low-sodium vegetable stock
1 cup (250 mL) dried couscous
2 medium tomatoes, finely chopped
1 fresh red cayenne chili, seeded and finely chopped
¼ cup (60 mL) finely chopped fresh parsley
¼ cup (60 mL) finely chopped fresh mint
2 Tbsp (30 mL) lemon juice
½ tsp (2 mL) sea salt
½ tsp (2 mL) freshly ground black pepper
2 Tbsp (30 mL) toasted pine nuts
1 Tbsp (15 mL) lemon zest

Place a medium saucepan over medium-high heat and add the oil, garlic, and shallot. Cook until softened, about 5 minutes. Add the cumin and vegetable stock, and bring to a boil. Remove the saucepan from the heat, stir in the couscous, cover, and set aside for 10 minutes or until all the liquid has been absorbed.

Combine the couscous, tomatoes, chili, parsley, mint, lemon juice, salt, and pepper in a large bowl and stir until well combined. Garnish with pine nuts and lemon zest, and chill before serving. Enjoy!

Serves 4 to 6
Prep time: 20 minutes
Cook time: 25 minutes

ROASTED BUTTERNUT SQUASH & APPLE SOUP

Butternut squash has a sweetness and robust nutty flavour that makes it an ideal comfort food. Roasting vegetables is a simple way of coaxing out every last bit of delicious flavour, and helps preserve their vitamins and minerals.

CORY'S TIPS

» There are many types of squash besides creamy-fleshed butternut, such as the fibre-rich acorn and the drier yet very tasty Hubbard. Most would work fine for this recipe.

» For extra warmth, add a little ground cayenne or dried red pepper flakes.

1 butternut squash (see tip), peeled, seeds removed, and roughly chopped in 1-inch (2.5 cm) cubes
1 Tbsp (15 mL) butter
1 large shallot, finely chopped
1 stalk celery, finely chopped
1 carrot, peeled and finely chopped
1 Granny Smith apple, peeled, cored, and roughly chopped
1 tsp (5 mL) sea salt
½ tsp (2 mL) freshly ground black pepper
¼ tsp (1 mL) ground cinnamon
¼ tsp (1 mL) ground nutmeg
3 cups (750 mL) low-sodium chicken stock
4 to 6 sprigs mint

Preheat the oven to 400°F (200°C). Place the squash on a large baking sheet and bake for 15 minutes.

Place a large saucepan on medium-high heat. Add the butter, shallot, celery, and carrot. Cook until the vegetables are soft, about 5 minutes. Add the roasted squash, sliced apple, salt, pepper, cinnamon, nutmeg, and chicken stock. Stir and bring to a boil. Reduce the heat and simmer for 3 minutes. Use an immersion blender, blender, or food processor to purée until smooth. Reheat if necessary. Pour into serving bowls and garnish each serving with a mint sprig.

Serves 4 to 6
Prep time: 25 minutes
Cook time: 3 hours

CRAZY PEA SOUP

This recipe was passed along to me by my friend Barbara Ann. When I was a child, pea soup was my least favourite soup, but I have come to really enjoy its complex flavours. If you feel as I did, perhaps it's time you gave it another try! This recipe is called crazy because I never thought I could come to love something I disliked so much as a child. Thanks again, Barbara Ann!

CORY'S TIPS

» To acquire a ham bone, check with your local grocer's meat department.
» A few drops of Angostura bitters add a special flavour to this soup.
» This soup freezes very well—I keep a few containers of it in my freezer to enjoy on a cold winter day.

1 gallon (4 L) water
5 cups (1.25 L) dried split peas
1 meaty ham bone
3 cups (750 mL) finely chopped shallots
2 tsp (10 mL) sea salt
1 tsp (5 mL) freshly ground black pepper
½ tsp (2 mL) dried marjoram
1 tsp (5 mL) Worcestershire sauce
2 cups (500 mL) finely chopped celery
2 cups (500 mL) peeled and finely chopped carrots
2 bay leaves

Place a large stockpot over medium-high heat, and bring the water and split peas to a boil. Simmer for 2 minutes, remove from the heat, and let stand covered for 1 hour.

Add the ham bone, shallots, salt, pepper, marjoram, and Worcestershire sauce. Bring to a boil. Reduce the heat and simmer for 1½ hours, stirring occasionally.

Remove the bone from the pot and let it cool. Take the meat off the bone, making sure to dice any large pieces of ham, and add the meat to the soup. Discard the bone. Add the celery, carrot, and bay leaves. Simmer over low heat, uncovered, for 30 to 40 minutes. Remove the bay leaves before serving.

Serves 4
Prep time: 10 minutes
Cook time: 20 minutes

SIMPLE GINGER-CARROT SOUP

Whenever I feel the winter blues or sniffles coming on, I head to the pantry and fight back with this soup. We've always been told that carrots are good for eyesight, and ginger, of course, is excellent for our immune system. And don't be fooled; just because this soup is simple doesn't mean it's boring! The avocado adds richness and fortifies this healthy soup with essential fatty acids, which we need for energy.

CORY'S TIPS

» If you are in a hurry, this soup is quick, easy, and very satisfying. And it freezes well!

» A little bit of ground coriander will contribute a wonderful earthy note.

1 Tbsp (15 mL) olive oil
6 large carrots, peeled and finely chopped
1 Tbsp (15 mL) grated fresh ginger
1 large ripe avocado, pitted, peeled, and thinly sliced
2 cups (500 mL) low-sodium vegetable stock
1 tsp (5 mL) sea salt
1 tsp (5 mL) freshly ground black pepper
¼ cup (60 mL) finely chopped cilantro

Place a large stockpot over medium-high heat and add the oil. Stir in the carrots and ginger, and cook until softened, about 5 minutes. Stir in the avocado, vegetable stock, salt, and pepper. Cook until the vegetables are very soft, about 10 minutes. Using an immersion blender or food processor, process until completely smooth. Reheat if necessary. Ladle into bowls and garnish each serving with some cilantro.

Serves 4
Prep time: 20 minutes
Cook time: 25 minutes

SPICY CURRIED SWEET POTATO SOUP

Sweet potatoes have become very popular in the past few years for their rich nutrients that make them a healthy source of carbohydrates. Sweet potatoes are a large component of my diet, and this soup in particular keeps them from becoming ho-hum. Their earthy sweetness combined with the Eastern flavours of curry and coriander makes this soup a fantastic escape from the everyday.

CORY'S TIPS

» A little dollop of sour cream or mascarpone cheese can add a special creaminess.

» I especially love the fresh ginger, and will add a little extra if I'm feeling a cold coming on. Ginger is excellent at supporting the immune system and helping to fight off colds.

2 Tbsp (30 mL) olive oil
1 cup (250 mL) finely chopped shallots
4 cups (1 L) peeled and chopped sweet potatoes
1 cup (250 mL) peeled and chopped carrots
1 tsp (5 mL) grated fresh ginger
1 tsp (5 mL) ground coriander
1 tsp (5 mL) madras curry powder
½ cup (125 mL) light coconut milk
4 cups (1 L) low-sodium vegetable stock
2 tsp (10 mL) sea salt
1 tsp (5 mL) freshly ground black pepper
1 Tbsp (15 mL) lemon juice
¼ cup (60 mL) finely chopped cilantro

Place a large saucepan over medium-high heat and add the olive oil and shallots. Cook until softened, about 5 minutes. Add the sweet potato and carrots, and cook until slightly softened, about 10 minutes. Stir in the ginger, coriander, and curry powder. Add the coconut milk and vegetable stock, and cook until the vegetables are very soft, about 10 minutes.

Use an immersion blender, food processor, or blender to process until the soup is very smooth. Reheat if necessary. Season with the salt, pepper, and lemon juice. Garnish each serving with the cilantro.

Serves 4
Prep time: 20 minutes
Cook time: 20 minutes

SPICY SUMMER ZUCCHINI SOUP

Anyone with even a small garden can feel overwhelmed by the amount of food it can produce! This soup is a fantastic way to enjoy and preserve these wonderful fresh flavours for any time of year. It freezes very well, so it's the perfect thing to bring a little summer sunshine to a cold, wintry day. It's very versatile, though—I also love to serve this cold on a hot summer's day with a nice glass of Chardonnay.

CORY'S TIPS

» Using a food processor or mandoline can speed up your prep time when preparing zucchini.
» If you just have too many zucchini to keep up with, contact your local food bank.

1 Tbsp (15 mL) olive oil
5 cloves garlic, finely chopped
2 shallots, finely chopped
1 Tbsp (15 mL) grated fresh ginger
1 tsp (5 mL) ground cayenne
1 tsp (5 mL) madras curry powder
2 lb (1 kg) zucchini, chopped
14 oz (398 mL) can light coconut milk
1 cup (250 mL) low-sodium chicken stock
¼ cup (60 mL) lime juice
1 tsp (5 mL) sea salt
½ cup (125 mL) light sour cream

Place a medium saucepan over medium-high heat, and add the oil, garlic, shallots, ginger, cayenne, and curry powder. Cook until soft, about 5 minutes. Add the zucchini, coconut milk, chicken stock, lime juice, and salt. Simmer until the zucchini is softened, about 10 minutes. Transfer the mixture to a food processor or blender and pulse until very smooth. Reheat if desired. Serve hot or cold with a dollop of sour cream.

Serves 4
Prep time: 20 minutes
Cook time: 25 minutes

ROASTED RED PEPPER & NEW POTATO SOUP

This recipe was inspired by my friend Mike, who loves to cook as much as I do. He and his wife served a soup like this at a dinner party, and it was an overwhelming success. Thanks again, Mike and Danielle, for the wonderful evening and the even better recipe inspiration!

CORY'S TIPS

» If you don't have time to roast your own red peppers, you can buy roasted red peppers in a jar.
» I once soft-poached an egg to garnish each serving. It added a wonderful richness and extra protein.
» If you like a little more heat, fresh cayenne chilies (seeded and finely chopped) can also be used to really bring this soup to life.

2 large red bell peppers
8 cups (2 L) low-sodium chicken stock
6 new potatoes, halved
3 cloves garlic, finely chopped
1 large shallot, finely chopped
1 cup (250 mL) milk
1 tsp (5 mL) sea salt
½ tsp (2 mL) ground cayenne
½ tsp (2 mL) freshly ground black pepper
2 Tbsp (30 mL) butter
1 tsp (5 mL) slivered dried chilies or chili flakes (optional)

Roast the bell peppers (whole) by placing under the broiler on a baking sheet. Turn frequently to blacken them on all sides, about 15 minutes. Place the peppers in a bowl, cover with plastic wrap, and allow to cool. Once cooled, peel off the blackened skin, remove the seeds, and cut the flesh into strips.

Place a large stockpot over medium-high heat, and add the chicken stock, sliced roasted peppers, potatoes, garlic, and shallot. Cook until the potatoes are soft, about 10 minutes. Add the milk, salt, cayenne, pepper, and butter. Use a blender or food processor to purée until smooth. Reheat if necessary and serve hot. Garnish with slivered dried chilies or chili flakes.

Serves 4
Prep time: 20 minutes
Cook time: 30 minutes

CORY'S CURRIED CAULIFLOWER CHILI SOUP

This soup has a wonderful creamy texture, and its Middle Eastern flavours make it both robust and satisfying. It can be served hot or cold, and makes a great second course for a dinner party.

CORY'S TIPS

» For extra depth of flavour, roast the cauliflower in a 400°F (200°C) oven for 15 to 20 minutes before adding it to the soup.

» For added richness, you could use buttermilk or even light cream instead of milk.

6 cups (1.5 L) roughly chopped cauliflower
1 cup (250 mL) peeled and chopped potatoes
3½ cups (875 mL) milk
1 fresh red cayenne chili, seeded and finely chopped
1 Tbsp (15 mL) ground coriander
1 tsp (5 mL) curry powder
1 tsp (5 mL) ground cumin
1 tsp (5 mL) sea salt
½ tsp (2 mL) freshly ground black pepper
2 Tbsp (30 mL) finely chopped chives

Place a medium saucepan over medium-high heat. Add the cauliflower, potatoes, and milk, and bring just to a boil. Reduce heat to medium. Add the chili, coriander, curry, cumin, salt, and pepper, and cook for 10 minutes. Reduce the heat further, cover, and simmer for 20 minutes or until tender.

Transfer to a food processor or blender, and pulse until smooth. Cover and refrigerate for 2 hours or until chilled. Thin with additional milk if desired. Garnish with the chives.

Serves 4
Prep time: 20 minutes
Cook time: 30 minutes

CHIPOTLE CARROT CORN CHOWDER

Wonderful as is—but for a little more sustenance you can add fish, chicken, or beef. Chowders can sometimes be a little bland, but not this one; it's a tasty combination of sweet fresh vegetables and smoky spice.

CORY'S TIPS

» For incredible added flavour, replace the corn niblets with two cobs of corn that you have roasted on your barbecue. Grill at 375°F (190°C) for 5 to 10 minutes, turning frequently. If you don't have a barbecue, roast the cobs in a preheated 400°F (200°C) oven for 5 to 10 minutes.

» Just a reminder: be sure to rinse leeks thoroughly, as they often have sand lodged within their leaves. Slice them in half lengthwise first so the water can get between all the layers.

» For a little added richness, substitute buttermilk or light cream for the low-fat milk.

1 tsp (5 mL) olive oil
1 shallot, finely chopped
1 leek, thinly sliced (white part only)
1½ cups (375 mL) vegetable stock
3 medium carrots, peeled and finely chopped
1 potato, peeled and finely chopped
1 sweet potato, peeled and finely chopped
½ cup (125 mL) coarsely chopped fresh parsley
1 Tbsp (15 mL) chipotle powder
1 tsp (5 mL) sea salt
1 tsp (5 mL) freshly ground black pepper
2 Tbsp (30 mL) all-purpose flour
1½ cups (375 mL) low-fat milk
1½ cups (375 mL) corn niblets (pre-thawed if frozen)
1 tsp (5 mL) dried thyme

Place a medium saucepan over medium-high heat, and add the olive oil, shallot, and leek. Cook until softened, 5 to 10 minutes. Add 1¼ cups (310 mL) of the vegetable stock, the carrots, potato, sweet potato, and ¼ cup (60 mL) of the parsley. Add the chipotle powder, salt, and pepper. Cover and simmer for 15 minutes or until tender.

Whisk the flour into the remaining ¼ cup (60 mL) of vegetable stock until smooth and stir into the soup. Add the milk and bring to a simmer, stirring occasionally. Add the corn, thyme, and remaining parsley. Simmer for 1 minute or until the soup has thickened to the desired consistency.

Serves 4
Prep time: 30 minutes
Cook time: 35 minutes

WILD FOREST MUSHROOM SOUP

I have always loved mushrooms, especially the wild varieties, and I have even had the privilege of accompanying a friend on mushroom-picking adventures. I highly recommend using a guide for these expeditions, as many varieties are poisonous, and can make you sick or even kill you! Of course, in the fall you can find fresh wild mushrooms in the local markets. I have used the dried variety in this recipe so you can make this dish at any time of year, but you can use the same amount of fresh mushrooms when you're lucky enough to find them.

CORY'S TIPS

» If using fresh wild mushrooms in this recipe, follow the directions, omitting the soaking mushrooms step. Mix the flour into an additional 2 cups (500 mL) chicken stock.
» If wild mushrooms are unavailable, white button or brown crimini mushrooms will work well.
» Fresh thyme sprigs add a nice earthy flavour—mushrooms and thyme have always been great friends.

4 cups (1 L) hot water
1 cup (250 mL) dried morel mushrooms
1 cup (250 mL) dried porcini mushrooms
1 cup (250 mL) dried chanterelle mushrooms
2 Tbsp (30 mL) butter
1 shallot, finely chopped
4 cloves garlic, finely chopped
5 Tbsp (75 mL) all-purpose flour
4 cups (1 L) low-sodium chicken stock
1 tsp (5 mL) sea salt
1 tsp (5 mL) freshly ground black pepper
½ cup (125 mL) whole milk
¼ cup (60 mL) finely chopped fresh parsley
¼ cup (60 mL) finely chopped chives

Place the hot water and dried mushrooms in a medium bowl and let soak for 30 minutes. Strain the mushrooms, reserving 2 cups (500 mL) of the liquid.

Place the butter, shallot, and garlic in a large saucepan over medium-high heat, and cook until softened, about 5 minutes. Add the drained, soaked mushrooms, cover, and simmer for 10 minutes.

Whisk the flour into the reserved mushroom liquid until thoroughly combined. Add the mixture and the chicken stock to the saucepan and bring to a boil. Reduce the heat and simmer for 20 minutes. Add the salt and pepper. Garnish each serving with a drizzle of milk and some chopped parsley and chives.

Serves 6 to 8
Prep time: 15 minutes
Cook time: 45 minutes

CREAMY CHORIZO & CHICKEN SOUP

It's really amazing how flavours can bring back some of our greatest memories. Whenever I want to take a trip, I simply open the refrigerator and the ingredients transport me to foreign lands. Chorizo sausage always takes me back to the southern part of Spain, where I stayed on a chicken farm. The ranchers called this soup *pollo poco loco,* or "crazy little chicken." This hearty soup makes a great main course.

CORY'S TIPS
» Chorizo works best here but nearly any sausage with the casing removed can be substituted.
» For the sake of health, this recipe calls for boneless, skinless chicken breasts, but I actually prefer using the dark thigh meat, as it is a little more flavourful.

2 Tbsp (30 mL) olive oil
1 Tbsp (15 mL) butter
4 boneless, skinless chicken breasts, cut in bite-sized pieces
2 Tbsp (30 mL) Worcestershire sauce
2 cloves garlic, finely chopped
1½ tsp (7.5 mL) sea salt
1 tsp (5 mL) freshly ground black pepper
1 lb (500 g) raw chorizo sausage, casings removed
4 cups (1 L) low-sodium chicken stock
28 oz (796 mL) can crushed tomatoes
1 cup (250 mL) light cream
½ cup (125 mL) shredded Monterey Jack cheese
½ cup (125 mL) grated Parmesan cheese
¼ cup (60 mL) light sour cream

Place a large stockpot over medium-high heat and add the olive oil and butter. Stir in the chicken, Worcestershire sauce, garlic, salt, and pepper. Cook until the chicken is no longer pink in the centre, about 10 minutes. Set aside on a plate.

Cook the chorizo sausage in the same stockpot until golden brown, about 10 minutes. Stir in the chicken stock, tomatoes, and reserved chicken. Reduce the heat to medium and simmer for 15 to 20 minutes. Add the cream, Monterey Jack, and Parmesan, and simmer another 5 minutes. Ladle into bowls and garnish each serving with a dollop of light sour cream.

Serves 4
Prep time: 15 minutes
Cook time: 35 minutes

CELERY CHICKEN GUMBO

This simple dish allows the ingredients to speak for themselves. Nothing needed, nothing missing. There's nothing like good old-fashioned chicken soup to chase away the flu, so the next time you're not feeling great and strong flavours aren't appealing, whip up a batch of this soup!

CORY'S TIPS

» For a twist, add freshly chopped coriander stalks to give the dish extra flavour and a crunchy texture.

» This recipe is great for those trying to control their food intake; celery packs a lot of flavour and is high in fibre, which helps to satiate appetite and aid digestion.

1 tsp (5 mL) olive oil
3 cups (750 mL) thinly sliced celery
1 cup (250 mL) finely chopped shallots
1 clove garlic, finely chopped
2 boneless, skinless chicken breasts, cut in bite-sized pieces
1 tsp (5 mL) sea salt
1 tsp (5 mL) freshly ground black pepper
2 cups (500 mL) low-sodium chicken stock
1 cup (250 mL) water
28 oz (796 mL) can diced tomatoes
½ cup (125 mL) long-grain brown basmati rice

Place a large saucepan over medium-high heat, and add the olive oil, celery, shallots, and garlic. Cook until softened, about 5 minutes. Add the chicken, and season with salt and pepper. Cook about 2 minutes or until the chicken is white all the way through, stirring occasionally. Stir in the chicken stock, water, tomatoes, and rice. Bring to a boil and reduce the heat. Cover and simmer until the rice is tender, 25 to 30 minutes.

Serves 6
Prep time: 30 minutes
Cook time: 35 minutes

THE BEST BOUILLABAISSE

This is another favourite, combining rich flavours and satisfying textures in a healthy dish. It is never inexpensive to make, and it does require a little extra work in the kitchen, but it's always worth it. I have found that it freezes quite well and gets even better with time. If you order this dish at a restaurant, expect to break the bank, so make it at home and freeze the leftovers. Then you can enjoy it a second and third time!

CORY'S TIPS

» To clean clams and mussels, scrub off any debris attached to the shells. It's also a good idea to soak shellfish in salted water in the refrigerator for a few hours to purge any sand inside the shells.

» When serving this dish, I like to line the bottom of each serving bowl with brown basmati rice and layer it with fresh spinach leaves. A couple of large spoonfuls of hot soup wilts the spinach, and the rice makes this dish very hearty and satisfying.

» Adding a little chopped fresh red cayenne chili doesn't hurt here, either, as it brings even more flavour to this dish.

¼ cup (60 mL) olive oil
4 large shallots, finely chopped
4 cloves garlic, finely chopped
4 stalks celery, finely chopped
1 red bell pepper, seeded and finely chopped
1 large bulb fennel, thinly sliced
two 28 oz (796 mL) cans diced tomatoes
3 sprigs fresh thyme
1 bay leaf
2 Tbsp (30 mL) orange zest
1 lb (500 g) halibut fillet, cut in bite-sized pieces
1 lb (500 g) fresh scallops
1 lb (500 g) large prawns, shelled and deveined
1 cup (250 mL) white wine
1 cup (250 mL) clam juice
2 Tbsp (30 mL) lemon juice
1 lb (500 g) fresh clams, cleaned
1 lb (500 g) fresh mussels, cleaned
½ lb (250 g) can lobster claw meat
½ tsp (2 mL) saffron
2 tsp (10 mL) sea salt
1 tsp (5 mL) freshly ground black pepper

Place a large stockpot over medium-high heat, and add the olive oil, shallots, garlic, celery, red pepper, and fennel. Cook until softened, about 5 minutes.

Reduce the heat to medium, and add the tomatoes, fresh thyme, bay leaf, and orange zest. Cook for 5 minutes. Add the halibut, scallops, prawns, white wine, clam juice, and lemon juice. Simmer for 10 minutes. Add the clams, mussels, and lobster meat. Cover and cook for 5 minutes, allowing the shellfish to steam.

Uncover and add the saffron, salt, and pepper. Simmer for an additional 5 minutes. Remove the bay leaf before serving.

VEGETABLE DISHES & PASTA

Serves 4
Prep time: 10 minutes
Cook time: 25 minutes

ASPARAGUS FRITTATA

Rise and shine! This frittata is an excellent way to start the day, with a hot cup of coffee, or Champagne and orange juice. I like to serve it to guests because it's quick to prepare and cook, which allows me more time to play host. Wouldn't you rather spend your morning visiting with friends than being stuck in the kitchen?

CORY'S TIPS
» Oka cheese is delicious here, but any cheese may be substituted.
» Leave the cherry tomatoes whole; it helps them keep their shape and prevents the juice from making your eggs runny.
» You can substitute sliced tomatoes for the cherry tomatoes, but put them on top of the cheese before broiling.

2 tsp (10 mL) olive oil
1 shallot, finely chopped
1 lb (500 g) asparagus spears, cut diagonally in 1-inch (2.5 cm) lengths
½ tsp (2 mL) sea salt
½ cup (125 mL) chopped fresh basil
½ tsp (2 mL) freshly ground black pepper
8 cherry tomatoes
8 large eggs, lightly beaten
1 cup (250 mL) shredded Oka cheese

Preheat the broiler. Place a large non-stick, ovenproof skillet over medium-high heat, and add the olive oil and shallot. Cook until softened, about 5 minutes. Add the asparagus, season with salt, and reduce the heat to medium-low. Cover and cook for 6 to 8 minutes.

Add the basil, pepper, and cherry tomatoes. Pour in the beaten eggs and cook until almost set, about 5 minutes. Top with the shredded cheese and place under the preheated broiler until the cheese is lightly browned, about 3 minutes.

Serves 4
Prep time: 10 minutes
Cook time: 40 minutes

PARIS ASPARAGUS & TOASTED PISTACHIO WILD RICE

The very first time I enjoyed this combination was in Paris, France. It was served alongside a beautiful piece of monkfish. You can serve it with any meaty fish; monkfish, halibut, and salmon all work beautifully. I found it appropriate that the asparagus was arranged to resemble the Eiffel tower, so I've done it that way too. I still introduce this dish to my friends as "the Paris Asparagus." Bon appétit!

CORY'S TIPS

» Use at least three asparagus spears for each serving to enable the vertical presentation.

» Toast the pistachios in a medium skillet over medium-high heat. Stir frequently and keep a close eye on them, as they do burn very quickly.

2 cups (500 mL) water
1 cup (250 mL) wild rice blend
1 tsp (5 mL) sea salt
¼ cup (60 mL) toasted pistachios
20 spears asparagus, woody ends snapped off
4 slices prosciutto
1 tsp (5 mL) freshly ground black pepper

Place a medium saucepan over medium-high heat, add the water, and bring to a boil. Add the rice and season with salt. Reduce the heat to a simmer and cook for 35 to 40 minutes or until all the water has been absorbed. Let stand for 5 minutes and fluff with a fork. Using a small bowl or ramekin to mould the rice, place a mound on each serving dish. Top with the toasted pistachios.

When rice timer has 20 minutes left, preheat the oven to 375°F (190°C). Wrap five asparagus spears in one slice of prosciutto and season with pepper. Finish all the bundles and place in an 11- × 7-inch (2 L) casserole dish. Cover with foil and bake in the centre of the oven for 20 minutes. Remove and stand each bundle vertically on a serving plate.

Serves 4 to 6
Prep time: 15 minutes
Cook time: 30 minutes

SPAGHETTI SQUASH WITH PEPPERS & PARMESAN

If you never thought your children would eat vegetables, just stand back and watch them devour this squash with long spaghetti-like strands. I have witnessed even the most finicky child asking for seconds. It pairs well with meats and fish, and freezes for use at a later date. I have even served this squash for breakfast with my Asparagus Frittata (page 83).

(page 83)

CORY'S TIPS

» When purchasing spaghetti squash, look for smooth, unblemished yellow skin.
» This squash can be difficult to cut, so put it in the microwave oven for a couple of minutes on high to soften the skin.

1 medium spaghetti squash, halved
½ cup (125 mL) grated Parmesan cheese
1 Tbsp (15 mL) butter
½ tsp (2 mL) sea salt
½ tsp (2 mL) freshly ground black pepper
½ cup (125 mL) finely chopped fresh basil
½ cup (125 mL) shredded mozzarella cheese
1 red bell pepper, seeded and finely sliced
2 Tbsp (30 mL) red wine

Preheat the oven to 350°F (180°C). Place the spaghetti squash cut side up in a 10- × 15-inch (4 L) casserole dish. Add 1 inch (2.5 cm) of water to the dish. Sprinkle ¼ cup (60 mL) Parmesan cheese in the squash halves. Dot with the butter and season with salt and pepper. Bake in the centre of the oven for 30 minutes or until the squash is tender.

Scoop the spaghetti-like flesh out of the skin and place in a large bowl. Toss with the basil, remaining ¼ cup (60 mL) Parmesan, mozzarella, red pepper, and wine. Enjoy!

Serves 4
Prep time: 15 minutes
Cook time: 20 minutes

SPICY SWEET POTATOES WITH FRESH GINGER

The sweet, spicy flavour of this dish gets me thinking of my grandmother. Instead of honey, she would add large marshmallows, which she called sugar pillows. Don't be afraid to experiment with the heat of fresh red cayenne chilies here (see Tips) because the potatoes' sweetness balances their spiciness. This dish fits in well at a traditional Christmas or Thanksgiving dinner. Just be sure to make more than you think you'll need—there are never any leftovers!

CORY'S TIPS

» Whenever possible I like to substitute fresh red cayenne chilies for ground cayenne, but it is only necessary to use half as much of the fresh; fresh chilies are much more potent than dried.

» Leave the skins on the sweet potatoes for a little bit more of a rustic feel, but be sure to scrub them thoroughly.

3 Tbsp (45 mL) butter
3 Tbsp (45 mL) olive oil
2 lb (1 kg) sweet potatoes, peeled and chopped
3 Tbsp (45 mL) grated fresh ginger
2 tsp (10 mL) chopped fresh thyme leaves
2 tsp (10 mL) ground allspice
3 cloves garlic, finely chopped
½ tsp (2 mL) sea salt
1 tsp (5 mL) ground cayenne
1 Tbsp (15 mL) honey

Place a medium saucepan over medium-high heat and add the butter, olive oil, and sweet potatoes. Cook the sweet potatoes until golden, about 10 minutes, stirring frequently. Stir in the ginger, thyme, allspice, garlic, salt, cayenne, and honey. Cook an additional 5 minutes until the sweet potatoes are fork tender.

Serves 4
Prep time: 10 minutes
Cook time: 15 minutes

NEW POTATOES WITH GARDEN-FRESH HERB VINAIGRETTE

This flavourful potato dish pairs beautifully with grilled meats such as Barbecued Tenderloin Steak with Crimini–Blue Cheese Sauce (page 134). For a switch, try to locate fingerling potatoes as they have a unique shape, creamy texture, and sweet flavour. If you know someone with a garden, see if you can barter a dinner cooked by you in exchange for some fresh produce—it will be well worth it!

CORY'S TIPS

» For a clean look on the plate, peel the cooked potatoes before dressing them.
» Golden oregano is one of my favourite herbs, and it adds a wonderful colour and exceptional flavour to dishes. I have had a golden oregano plant in my garden for the past ten years. Look for it in the herb section at your local nursery. If golden oregano is not available, use any type of fresh oregano.
» I use the white balsamic vinegar because it won't colour the potatoes, but regular balsamic will work just fine.

2 lb (1 kg) new potatoes, washed and halved
2 tsp (10 mL) sea salt
¼ cup (60 mL) extra virgin olive oil
¼ cup (60 mL) lemon juice
1 Tbsp (15 mL) white balsamic vinegar
1 tsp (5 mL) Dijon mustard
2 Tbsp (30 mL) finely chopped fresh basil
1 Tbsp (15 mL) finely chopped fresh golden oregano
2 tsp (10 mL) chopped fresh thyme leaves
1 tsp (5 mL) freshly ground black pepper
1 shallot, finely chopped

Place potatoes in a medium saucepan and add enough cold water to cover by 1 inch (2.5 cm). Bring to a boil and season with 1 tsp (5 mL) of the salt. Simmer for 6 to 8 minutes, or until the potatoes are fork tender.

While the potatoes are cooking, make the vinaigrette. Whisk the olive oil, lemon juice, vinegar, mustard, basil, oregano, thyme, remaining 1 tsp (5 mL) salt, pepper, and shallot together in a medium bowl.

When the potatoes are cooked, drain and toss gently in the vinaigrette. Serve warm or chilled.

Serves 4 to 6
Prep time: 15 minutes
Cook time: 45 minutes

VEGETABLE CASSEROLE

This recipe is straight out of my grandmother's family cookbook and has been served at nearly all our family functions. For your almost-vegetarian guests who eat eggs, this dish delivers hearty flavour. Depending on the season, substitute or add other vegetables, such as sweet potato, which provides a smooth texture and sweetness that enhances the other vegetables.

CORY'S TIP

» For non-vegetarians, you can make this into a very hearty meal by adding cooked and cubed beef or chicken to this already tasty dish.

2 cups (500 mL) chopped broccoli
2 cups (500 mL) chopped zucchini
2 cups (500 mL) corn niblets
2 cups (500 mL) chopped shallots
2 cups (500 mL) chopped red bell pepper
2 cups (500 mL) chopped celery
1½ cups (375 mL) shredded cheddar cheese
3 eggs
1¼ cups (310 mL) milk
1 cup (250 mL) Bisquick
1 tsp (5 mL) sea salt
1 tsp (5 mL) freshly ground black pepper

Preheat the oven to 400°F (200°C). Put the broccoli, zucchini, corn, shallots, bell peppers, and celery in a 10- × 15-inch (4 L) casserole dish. Top with the shredded cheese.

Whisk the eggs, milk, Bisquick, salt, and pepper in a medium bowl. Pour over the vegetables. Bake in the centre of the oven for 35 to 45 minutes.

Serves 4
Prep time: 10 minutes
Cook time: 15 minutes

PENNE WITH TOMATO & FETA

If you've been to Italy or have an Italian background, you will recognize this traditional dish that is both delicious and beautiful. In my travels I found that Italians are very patriotic, and this dish is a salute to their culture, and even to their red, white, and green flag. For still more Italian colours, serve this with my Fresh Tomato, Basil, & Bocconcini Salad (page 51). *Viva l'Italia*!

CORY'S TIPS

» To give the dish a creamier texture, add bocconcini cheese.

» Some shredded fresh basil makes a nice garnish.

» Any form of pasta may be used in place of the penne. My favourite variation is radiatore because it has many small grooves to capture the flavourful ingredients.

1 gallon (4 L) water
2 tsp (10 mL) sea salt
1 lb (500 g) uncooked penne
1 Tbsp (15 mL) olive oil
1 clove garlic, finely chopped
4 large tomatoes, chopped
½ cup (125 mL) crumbled feta cheese
½ cup (125 mL) finely chopped fresh parsley
2 Tbsp (30 mL) chopped fresh basil
1 tsp (5 mL) freshly ground black pepper
½ cup (125 mL) grated Parmesan cheese

Bring the water and salt to a boil in a large stockpot over medium-high heat. Add the penne and return to a boil. Cook for 7 to 9 minutes until al dente. Drain and set aside.

Place a large saucepan over medium-high heat and add the olive oil and garlic. Cook until softened, about 3 minutes. Add the tomatoes and cook for about 3 minutes or until heated through. Transfer the drained pasta to the saucepan and add the feta, parsley, basil, and pepper. Toss gently and garnish each serving with fresh Parmesan.

Serves 4
Prep time: 15 minutes
Cook time: 25 minutes

WILD BUFFALO PENNE

Buffalo, or bison as it is also called, has become very popular in the last few years and for good reason. The meat is lean and full-flavoured without having a gamy flavour. It is free of steroids and antibiotics, making it a good option for the health conscious, and it is a sustainable food source. Not only does it make fantastic barbecued burgers, it's a great way to support local farmers. Pair this dish with my Crispy Prosciutto & Artichoke Salad (page 52), and serve with a full-bodied red wine for a delightful meal.

CORY'S TIP

» To locate an organic farm that sells bison in your area, check on the Internet or ask at your local specialty meats shop. It is slightly more expensive than regular ground beef, but the lack of hormones and drug residues and the rich flavour far outweigh the difference in cost.

1 gallon (4 L) water
2 tsp (10 mL) sea salt
1 lb (500 g) uncooked penne
1 Tbsp (15 mL) olive oil
1 lb (500 g) ground buffalo
1 shallot, finely chopped
1 tsp (5 mL) red pepper flakes
1 tsp (5 mL) sea salt
¼ cup (60 mL) chopped celery
28 oz (796 mL) can crushed tomatoes
2 Tbsp (30 mL) Worcestershire sauce
¼ cup (60 mL) chopped fresh parsley

Bring a large stockpot with the water to a boil over high heat and add the 2 tsp (10 mL) salt. Add the pasta and cook for 8 to 10 minutes or until al dente. Drain and set aside.

While the penne is cooking, place a medium saucepan over medium-high heat and add the olive oil and ground buffalo. Cook until browned, about 10 minutes. Remove the meat from the saucepan and set it aside.

Add the chopped shallot to the same saucepan and cook until softened, about 5 minutes. Add the red pepper flakes, remaining salt, and browned buffalo. Stir in the celery, tomatoes, and Worcestershire sauce. Reduce the heat and let simmer for 5 minutes. Mix in the cooked penne and parsley, and simmer for an additional 5 minutes. Garnish with a little grated fresh Parmesan and freshly ground black pepper to taste.

Serves 4
Prep time: 15 minutes
Cook time: 20 minutes

CORY'S CAPELLINI CARBONARA

I recommend using capellini (or angel hair pasta, which is even thinner) for this dish because its delicate texture holds the sauce well. This recipe may seem a little cheesy, and, well . . . it is! Taste this dish prior to adding any extra salt, as the pancetta is quite high in sodium. Let your taste buds be your guide when it comes to the seasoning of any dish. I often prepare my Escargots in Crimini Mushroom Caps (page 24) as a starter for this dish.

CORY'S TIP

» Be sure to drain the pasta while it is still al dente, as it will continue to cook slightly in the saucepan.

1 gallon (4 L) water
2 tsp (10 mL) sea salt
1 lb (500 g) uncooked capellini
10 oz (300 g) pancetta cut in ½-inch (1 cm) dice
4 egg yolks
1 cup (250 mL) light cream
2 cups (500 mL) grated Parmesan cheese
½ tsp (2 mL) freshly ground black pepper

Bring a large stockpot with the water to a boil over high heat. Season with the salt and add the pasta. Cook pasta for 6 to 8 minutes until al dente.

While the pasta is cooking, place a medium saucepan over medium-high heat and add the pancetta. Cook until browned, about 5 minutes. In a medium bowl combine the egg yolks, cream, 1½ cups (375 mL) of the grated Parmesan, and pepper.

Drain the pasta and add to the saucepan with the pancetta. Remove from the heat and immediately stir in the cheese mixture, and toss well. Garnish with the remaining ½ cup (125 mL) of grated Parmesan cheese.

Serves 4
Prep time: 15 minutes
Cook time: 15 minutes

SMOKED SALMON BOWTIE PASTA

This recipe came to me from an excellent chef who loves food even more than I do. It's easy to prepare and takes next to no time to cook. Some days you may not feel like making a big production out of dinner, and for those days, this quick, simple recipe is perfect. Strawberry Spinach Salad (page 50) is a wonderful starter to this very flavourful dish.

CORY'S TIPS

» If fresh herbs are unavailable, use dried ones instead. But reduce the amount of dried herbs by half because dried herbs have a more concentrated flavour.
» Another thing I adore adding here is drained capers—their flavour works very well with salmon.
» Make sure to undercook your pasta slightly, as it will cook a little more with the sauce, and overcooked pasta is just plain horrible!

1 gallon (4 L) water
2 tsp (2 mL) sea salt
1 lb (500 g) uncooked farfalle (bowtie pasta)
2 Tbsp (30 mL) olive oil
¼ cup (60 mL) finely chopped shallots
2 cloves garlic, finely chopped
1 Tbsp (15 mL) lemon juice
1 Tbsp (15 mL) lemon zest
¼ cup (60 mL) white wine
¼ cup (60 mL) light cream
10 oz (300 g) smoked salmon, cut in bite-sized
    pieces
2 Tbsp (30 mL) finely chopped fresh parsley
1 Tbsp (15 mL) finely chopped fresh dill
½ tsp (2 mL) freshly ground black pepper

Bring a large stockpot with the water to a boil over high heat and add the salt. Add the pasta and cook at a vigorous boil for 8 to 10 minutes or until al dente. Drain the pasta, reserving 1 cup (250 mL) of the cooking liquid.

While the pasta is cooking, place a large saucepan over medium-high heat and add the olive oil, shallots, and garlic. Cook until softened, about 5 minutes. Add the lemon juice, zest, and white wine, and continue cooking until reduced by one-half. Add the cream and simmer for an additional minute. Remove from the heat.

Add the pasta to the sauce. Stir in a little of the reserved cooking liquid if it is too dry. Gently stir in the smoked salmon, parsley, dill, and pepper.

Serves 4
Prep time: 15 minutes
Cook time: 30 minutes

BOWTIES DEL CORAY

The inspiration for this pasta recipe comes from a little restaurant here in Nanaimo. It is very simple to prepare and the flavours are amazing. This is my version of this dish and it is so good that I put my name on it!

CORY'S TIPS

» Sun-dried tomatoes packed in oil are best for this recipe as they are ready to use and do not require rehydrating. Specialty delis and import markets often carry snow goat cheese, but if it is difficult to find, any soft goat cheese is an excellent substitute.

» Double your garlic quotient by adding a bulb of roasted garlic to this dish (page 19). Simply squeeze the cloves directly into the pasta with your other seasonings.

» I like the bowtie pasta for this dish, but any shape may be used.

1 gallon (4 L) water
2 tsp (10 mL) sea salt
1 lb (500 g) uncooked farfalle (bowtie pasta)
1 Tbsp (15 mL) olive oil
2 cloves garlic, finely chopped
1 shallot, finely chopped
2 boneless, skinless chicken breasts, cubed
3 oz (90 g) sun-dried tomatoes, finely chopped
7 oz (200 g) crumbled snow goat cheese
1 cup (250 mL) roughly chopped fresh parsley
6 slices prosciutto, finely chopped
1 tsp (5 mL) sea salt
1 tsp (5 mL) freshly ground black pepper

Bring a large stockpot with the water to a boil over high heat. Season with 2 tsp (10 mL) salt. Add the pasta and cook for 8 to 10 minutes or until al dente. Drain and set aside.

Place a large saucepan over medium-high heat and add the olive oil, garlic, and shallot. Cook until softened, about 5 minutes. Add the chicken and cook until opaque, about 10 minutes. Add the sun-dried tomatoes and cook an additional 5 minutes. Combine the cooked pasta with the chicken and stir in the goat cheese, parsley, prosciutto, 1 tsp (5 mL) salt, and pepper.

FISH & SEAFOOD

Serves 4
Prep time: 10 minutes
Cook time: 15 minutes

CORY'S GREEN COCONUT CURRY WITH PRAWNS

Invite some of your best friends over to help devour this delicious dish. Food is always more fun when you share it with friends, and they can help you clean up! When I make this, I like to use the largest prawns I can find. Pair it with Paris Asparagus & Toasted Pistachio Wild Rice (page 84) for a wonderful meal.

CORY'S TIP

» Simmer the sauce to the desired thickness (the longer you simmer, the thicker it will become) before you add the prawns. Prawns cook quickly and will become very tough if overdone.

1 Tbsp (15 mL) olive oil
1 shallot, finely chopped
2 cloves garlic, finely chopped
1 tsp (5 mL) sea salt
1 tsp (5 mL) freshly ground black pepper
3 Tbsp (45 mL) garam masala
1 Tbsp (15 mL) green curry paste
14 oz (398 mL) can light coconut milk
2 lb (1 kg) prawns, shelled and deveined
1 Tbsp (15 mL) chopped fresh cilantro

Place a medium saucepan over medium heat and add the olive oil, shallot, garlic, salt, pepper, and garam masala. Cook until garlic and shallot is softened, about 5 minutes. Add the green curry paste and coconut milk, and bring to a gentle simmer. Cook for 5 minutes, stirring occasionally. Add the prawns and cook for 5 minutes or until they are pink. Garnish with fresh cilantro.

Serves 4
Prep time: 10 minutes
Cook time: 10 minutes

WEST COAST GRILLED PRAWN PIZZA

Barbecued pizza? I first had it in Seville, Spain, and when I saw it on the menu I thought the chef was totally crazy. But when I tasted his perfectly grilled pizza, I was impressed. I think every pizza should be grilled, and this is my rendition of the perfect grilled pizza. Store-bought pizza will never come close to this one!

CORY'S TIP

» Frozen pizza dough is available at supermarkets, but also check your local pizza parlor to see if they sell their own pizza dough frozen.

2 Tbsp (30 mL) olive oil
2 Tbsp (30 mL) cornmeal
1 lb (500 g) prepared pizza dough (fresh, or frozen and thawed)
¼ cup (60 mL) store-bought pesto
2 shallots, finely chopped
2 cups (500 mL) baby spinach
5 oz (150 g) crumbled goat cheese
8 cherry tomatoes, halved
1 large ripe avocado, pitted, peeled, and sliced
16 medium prawns, shelled and deveined
1 tsp (5 mL) sea salt
1 tsp (5 mL) freshly ground black pepper

Heat the grill to medium-high. Brush a large baking sheet with 1 Tbsp (15 mL) of the olive oil. Lightly dust your work surface with cornmeal. Divide the dough in half, and roll and stretch it into two 10-inch (25 cm) rounds. Transfer to the baking sheet and brush the tops with the remaining 1 Tbsp (15 mL) of olive oil.

Carefully place the dough directly on the grill and cook for 2 to 3 minutes or until the undersides begin to brown slightly. Remove from the grill and use tongs or a big spatula to flip the dough. Spread the pesto over the grilled sides of both pizzas and spread out with the back of a spoon. Evenly distribute the shallots, spinach, goat cheese, tomato halves, avocado, prawns, salt, and pepper over the surface of both pizzas. Return to the grill and cook with the lid down for approximately 5 minutes or until the cheese is melted and the prawns are cooked.

Serves 4
Prep time: 15 minutes
Cook time: 25 minutes

GRILLED SWORDFISH WITH CHAMPAGNE SAUCE

I love the firm texture and mild flavour of swordfish, but it's rather expensive, so I reserve it for special occasions. The fantastic richness of this simple dish pairs well with fresh seasonal vegetables and wild rice. Or serve it with the vegetable linguini from Baked Salmon Fillet with Vegetable Linguini (page 106).

CORY'S TIPS

» If swordfish is unavailable, ahi tuna, mahi mahi, or any other firm fish makes a good substitute.

» I have made this dish for numerous special occasions using Champagne, but I have also had success substituting a dry white wine for more casual events.

1 cup (250 mL) Champagne
2 Tbsp (30 mL) fresh orange juice
½ cup (125 mL) butter
2 Tbsp (30 mL) light cream
Four 6 oz (175 g) swordfish steaks
1 Tbsp (15 mL) olive oil
1 tsp (5 mL) sea salt
1 tsp (5 mL) freshly ground black pepper

Preheat the barbecue to 350°F (180°C). Place the Champagne and orange juice in a medium saucepan over medium heat. Cook until mixture is reduced by one-third, about 15 minutes. Remove from the heat and stir in the butter until melted. Gently stir in the cream.

Lightly brush the steaks with olive oil and season with salt and pepper. Grill the steaks on the barbecue for approximately 4 minutes per side.

To serve, plate the swordfish and pour the sauce over the steaks.

Serves 4
Prep time: 15 minutes
Cook time: 10 minutes

BARRAMUNDI FILLET WITH SPICY MANGO & BASIL SALSA

I particularly enjoy this dish during the hot summer months; it's tasty and light with a hint of heat. Barramundi is sweet, mild, and moist, and has a buttery flavour. It's also high in omega-3 fatty acids. If you've never tried it, I guarantee you'll find a new favourite! Serve this with fresh seasonal vegetables and wild rice.

CORY'S TIPS

» You can use thin fillets of ling cod, sole, or red snapper instead of the barramundi.
» Sambal oelek is available in the import sections of most grocery stores, and delicatessens and specialty food shops often carry this item.
» Make the salsa the night before to save time and allow all the flavours to blend together.

Four 5 oz (150 g) barramundi fillets
1 cup (250 mL) milk
1 cup (250 mL) panko (Japanese breadcrumbs)
1 tsp (5 mL) sea salt
1 tsp (5 mL) freshly ground black pepper
1 Tbsp (15 mL) olive oil
1 Tbsp (15 mL) butter
1 mango, peeled and finely chopped
½ cup (125 mL) chopped fresh basil
1 Tbsp (15 mL) sambal oelek

Pat the barramundi fillets dry with paper towels. Pour the milk into a shallow bowl. Combine the panko, salt, and pepper on a large plate and mix well. Dip the fillets in milk and then coat with the seasoned panko.

Place a medium skillet over medium-high heat and add the olive oil and butter. Carefully place the fillets in the pan and cook until golden brown on both sides, approximately 2 minutes per side. Set aside on individual serving plates.

Combine the mango, basil, and sambal oelek in a small bowl. Spoon on top of the barramundi fillets and serve immediately.

Serves 4
Prep time: 25 minutes
Cook time: 20 minutes

BAKED SALMON FILLET WITH VEGETABLE LINGUINI

This recipe is always a summer hit, and the fact that the vegetables look like pasta noodles can help satisfy cravings for the starchy stuff, without the starch! This dish pairs very well with a light white wine and nice, soft focaccia bread.

CORY'S TIP

» This recipe is an excellent way to get your kids to eat their vegetables! If they like to help in the kitchen, vegetable peelers are relatively safe and allow them an opportunity to get in on the fun.

2 large carrots
1 large zucchini
1 large sweet potato
Four 7 oz (200 g) salmon fillets
2 tsp (10 mL) sea salt
1 tsp (5 mL) freshly ground black pepper
½ cup (125 mL) light coconut milk
½ cup (125 mL) non-fat yogurt
¼ cup (60 mL) finely chopped shallots
2 Tbsp (30 mL) miso paste
¼ tsp (1 mL) freshly ground nutmeg
¼ tsp (1 mL) freshly ground black pepper
2 cups (500 mL) broccoli florets

Preheat the oven to 350°F (180°C). Peel the carrots, zucchini, and sweet potato. Cut the zucchini in half and discard the seeds. Use a vegetable peeler to create long strips of each vegetable (they should look like linguini noodles). Set aside.

Place the salmon fillets on a rimmed baking sheet, skin side down, and season with salt and pepper. Bake in the centre rack of the oven for 12 to 15 minutes or until the fillets are firm to the touch.

While the fish is baking, whisk together the coconut milk, yogurt, shallots, miso, nutmeg, and pepper in a bowl until thoroughly combined. Transfer to a large stockpot over medium-high heat. Add the vegetable strips and broccoli crowns, cover, and cook for 6 to 8 minutes. Plate the salmon fillets alongside your vegetable linguini and serve.

Serves 4
Prep time: 10 minutes
Cook time: 30 minutes

SPICY MAPLE SYRUP–GLAZED SALMON

I was given this recipe by a First Nations friend who has a great passion for cooking and maintaining some of the traditional methods of his culture. This is one of his favourites and has become one of mine as well. I was impressed when he served this with a nice piece of warm bannock. Other good accompaniments are wild rice and seasonal vegetables. Shrimp, Cucumber, & Watermelon Salad (page 57) is a wonderful starter for this dish.

CORY'S TIPS

» You can use hard apple cider, but be sure to cook the glaze for 3 to 5 minutes longer to remove the alcohol.
» Vacuum-sealed salmon fillets keep very well in the freezer, offering the opportunity to have this summer treat even during winter months.
» Remember to use the real maple syrup here, not the fake pancake stuff!

¾ cup (185 mL) fresh apple cider
2 Tbsp (30 mL) maple syrup
1 fresh red cayenne chili, seeded and finely chopped
Four 7 oz (200 g) skinless salmon fillets
½ tsp (2 mL) sea salt
½ tsp (2 mL) freshly ground black pepper
1 tsp (5 mL) olive oil
1 Tbsp (15 mL) butter
4 lemon wedges

Place a medium saucepan over medium-high heat and add the apple cider, maple syrup, and chili. Bring the mixture to a boil and continue cooking to reduce it by one-third, about 15 minutes.

Preheat the oven to 350°F (180°C). Place the salmon in a single layer in a 10- × 15-inch (4 L) baking dish and pour the mixture over the salmon. Set aside for 10 minutes.

Season the salmon with the salt and pepper. Place a large ovenproof skillet over medium-high heat and heat the olive oil and butter in it. Add the salmon fillets and cook for 2 minutes per side, brushing frequently with the cider glaze. Squeeze the lemon wedges over the fillets. Place the pan in the centre of the preheated oven and bake for 8 to 10 minutes.

Serves 4
Prep time: 10 minutes
Cook time: 20 minutes

SMOKY CEDAR-PLANKED SALMON

I can clearly remember the first time I made this dish. I neglected to note that planked salmon is to be cooked over indirect heat and not directly over the flames of a grill. With the lid closed, I simply thought I was getting a nice smoked fish. I couldn't have been more wrong! Try serving a planked salmon when the plank is on fire! Can you say *salmon flambé*? You will need four individual serving–sized cedar planks for this. They need to be thoroughly soaked overnight, so don't forget to do this the night before. Paris Asparagus & Toasted Pistachio Wild Rice (page 84) is a great accompaniment for this salmon.

CORY'S TIPS

» Ask your fishmonger to remove the skin and pin bones from the salmon to make preparing this dish easier.

» Look for fish that doesn't smell "fishy," but rather just lightly of the ocean.

» If you don't have access to sockeye or prefer another type of salmon, just use your favourite.

» I have found lemon ginger oil at the local seafood market and have also seen it at some specialty food shops. If you can't find it, you can make it yourself by combining 2 Tbsp (30 mL) lemon juice, 2 tsp (10 mL) grated fresh ginger, and 1 Tbsp (15 mL) olive oil.

Four 7 oz (200 g) sockeye salmon fillets
4 tsp (20 mL) lemon ginger oil (see Tip)
1 tsp (5 mL) finely chopped fresh dill
2 Tbsp (30 mL) capers, drained
1 Tbsp (15 mL) lemon zest
1 tsp (5 mL) sea salt
1 tsp (5 mL) freshly ground black pepper

Preheat the barbecue to 350°F (180°C). Place the salmon on the soaked cedar planks and drizzle with the lemon ginger oil. Sprinkle with the dill, capers, and lemon zest. Season with the salt and pepper. Grill over indirect heat, using only one burner (absolutely no flames under your cedar planks!), for 20 minutes or until the fish is firm to the touch. Carefully remove the planks from the barbecue, but serve the fish right off the plank.

Serves 4
Prep time: 20 minutes
Cook time: 15 minutes

MANGO CURRY SALMON FILLETS

Sweet, firm-textured mango and curry are fabulous partners. Make this in summer, when mangoes are at their best and fresh salmon is abundant. Accompany it with Paris Asparagus & Toasted Pistachio Wild Rice (page 84). Served with a cool, crisp white wine on a hot summer's evening—perfection!

CORY'S TIPS

» If mangoes aren't in season, try fresh papaya or even ripe plums.
» If you enjoy a little taste of the Caribbean, add 2 Tbsp (30 mL) of dark rum to your sauce and simmer gently for 5 minutes to incorporate the flavours.
» Cane sugar may be substituted for brown sugar for an exotic sweetness.
» If cilantro is unavailable, use 1 tsp (5 mL) dried coriander.
» I always enjoy adding a little fresh cayenne chili, which brings out all the savoury sweetness of the dish.

Four 6 oz (175 g) salmon fillets
2 Tbsp (30 mL) olive oil
3 Tbsp (45 mL) lime juice
1 tsp (5 mL) sea salt
1 tsp (5 mL) freshly ground black pepper
14 oz (398 mL) can light coconut milk
1 Tbsp (15 mL) soy sauce
2 tsp (10 mL) brown sugar
1 tsp (5 mL) cornstarch
1 tsp (5 mL) curry powder
½ ripe mango, peeled and finely chopped
2 Tbsp (30 mL) chopped cilantro

Preheat the oven to 425°F (220°C). Line a rimmed 10- × 15-inch (25 × 38 cm) baking sheet with parchment paper and place the salmon in the pan. Drizzle with the oil and 2 Tbsp (30 mL) of the lime juice. Season with the salt and pepper. Place in the centre of the oven and bake for 12 to 14 minutes until firm to the touch and cooked through.

While the salmon is baking, make the sauce. Place a small pot over medium heat and whisk together the remaining 1 Tbsp (15 mL) lime juice, coconut milk, soy sauce, brown sugar, cornstarch, and curry powder. Add the mango. Simmer gently for 10 minutes, stirring occasionally. Stir in the cilantro. Plate the salmon fillets and pour the sauce overtop.

Serves 4
Prep time: 15 minutes
Cook time: 15 minutes

PANKO-CRUSTED SALMON

The panko breading in this recipe helps keep the salmon moist and tender. I eat salmon on a regular basis for health reasons—it's a great source of healthy omega-3 fatty acids. I especially enjoy serving this dish to friends from out of town who don't have regular access to fresh salmon. My salmon is so fresh it arrives at my door only minutes after being taken out of the water!

CORY'S TIP

» I have used both halibut and chicken breasts instead of salmon in this recipe with wonderful results. If you buy skinless salmon fillets, it's more convenient, but the skin adds a little extra flavour. To serve, just slip a large spatula carefully between the fillet and the skin, and the fillet will come off evenly in one piece.

Four 7 oz (200 g) salmon fillets
2 tsp (10 mL) sea salt
½ tsp (2 mL) freshly ground black pepper
2 Tbsp (30 mL) sweet hot mustard
1 Tbsp (15 mL) honey
2 tsp (10 mL) chopped fresh thyme leaves
2 Tbsp (30 mL) lemon juice
1 cup (250 mL) panko (Japanese breadcrumbs)
4 tsp (20 mL) olive oil
2 Tbsp (30 mL) chopped fresh parsley
½ tsp (2 mL) sweet hot paprika

Preheat the oven to 400°F (200°C). Place the salmon on a large, rimmed baking sheet with the skin side down. Pat the salmon dry with paper towels to help the panko crust adhere more evenly. Season with the salt and pepper. In a small bowl, combine the mustard, honey, 1 tsp (5 mL) of the thyme, and lemon juice. In another small bowl, mix the panko with the remaining 1 tsp (5 mL) thyme, olive oil, parsley, and paprika.

Spread the mustard mixture on the salmon. Top with the panko mixture, pressing it on evenly with your hands to form a crust. Bake the salmon for 12 to 14 minutes or until firm to the touch.

Serves 4
Prep time: 20 minutes
Cook time: 15 minutes

PANKO-BREADED HALIBUT WITH FLAMED PERNOD FENNEL & PEPPER SALAD

This dish is a crowd-pleaser at any party because there's something really exciting about flames in your kitchen (as long as they are intentional). Most any white fish could be used in this recipe, and your fishmonger should be able to provide you with a boneless, skinless fillet upon request.

CORY'S TIPS

» Tarragon is a lovely addition to this dish, adding yet more licorice flavour (in addition to that of the fennel). It is very powerful whether fresh or dried, so use it sparingly.

» Keep an eye on the halibut when cooking, as panko browns very quickly.

Four 7 oz (200 g) halibut fillets
½ cup (125 mL) all-purpose flour
1 egg, beaten
8 oz (227 g) box panko (Japanese breadcrumbs)
1 tsp (5 mL) sea salt
1 tsp (5 mL) freshly ground black pepper
2 Tbsp (30 mL) olive oil
2 bulbs fennel, thinly sliced
½ cup (125 mL) Pernod
1 red bell pepper, julienned
1 yellow bell pepper, julienned
1 Tbsp (15 mL) butter

Dry the halibut with paper towels. Place the flour, beaten egg, and panko on three separate plates. Coat the halibut in the flour, shaking off any excess. Next, dredge the halibut in the beaten egg and then thoroughly coat in the panko. Season with the salt and pepper and set aside.

Place a large saucepan over medium-high heat and add 1 Tbsp (15 mL) of the olive oil, and the fennel. Cook until slightly softened, about 5 minutes. Add the Pernod and carefully ignite. When the flames have diminished, add the bell peppers and continue to cook for 5 to 7 minutes.

Place a separate medium skillet over medium-high heat and add the remaining 1 Tbsp (15 mL) olive oil and the butter. Carefully add the halibut. Cook, rotating the pieces until they are golden brown on all sides, about 2 minutes per side. Divide the fennel salad among four plates and top with the halibut. Enjoy!

Serves 4 to 6
Prep time: 15 minutes
Cook time: 15 minutes

MANGO HALIBUT TACOS

This recipe is a lot of fun for a group of friends who enjoy visiting and creating dinner together. I have even prepared this recipe for a friend's tenth birthday party. I prefer to use halibut in this dish because of its firm texture and wonderful flavour, although any type of fish may be used.

CORY'S TIPS

» Any type of tortilla or taco shell can be used in this recipe, although I enjoy whole wheat flour tortillas the most.
» If mangoes are unavailable, try creating something completely different by using grilled pineapple, papaya, or even dragon fruit!

1¼ lb (625 g) halibut fillet
2 Tbsp (30 mL) olive oil
2 Tbsp (30 mL) lime juice
2 Tbsp (30 mL) brown sugar
1 tsp (5 mL) chili powder
1 tsp (5 mL) ground cumin
¼ tsp (1 mL) ground cayenne
1 tsp (5 mL) sea salt
1 tsp (5 mL) freshly ground black pepper
8 medium-sized whole wheat flour tortillas, warmed
1½ cups (375 mL) shredded romaine or head lettuce
1 cup (250 mL) tomato salsa
1 ripe mango, peeled and finely chopped

Preheat the oven to 425°F (220°C) and line a large, rimmed baking sheet with parchment paper. Remove the skin from the halibut and cut the fish into 1- × ¼-inch (2.5 × 0.5 cm) strips. In a medium bowl, combine the olive oil, lime juice, sugar, chili powder, cumin, cayenne, and halibut strips. Arrange the halibut pieces on the baking sheet in a single layer and season with the salt and pepper. Bake for 8 to 10 minutes or until cooked through. Place the halibut on a serving plate and invite everyone to build their own tacos with the tortillas, lettuce, salsa, and mango. Enjoy!

Serves 4
Prep time: 10 minutes
Cook time: 25 minutes

GRILLED-HALIBUT TACOS WITH HOT CHILI SALSA

This fantastic recipe is definitely for those who love spicy food, though the heat does mellow with cooking. The first year I grew habañero chilies is something I will never forget. A little sample of raw pepper from a plant and I was sent screaming across the yard. I've always liked very hot food—just not that hot! Habañeros have excellent flavour and pack tons of heat. No wonder their nickname is Tasmanian devil!

CORY'S TIPS
» When you buy the halibut, ask your fishmonger to remove the skin.
» A word of caution: when using habañero chilies, DON'T TOUCH YOUR EYES! Or anything else, for that matter. I recommend wearing rubber gloves whenever working with chilies, just as a precaution.

2 poblano chilies
1 jalapeño chili
1 habañero chili
1 avocado, pitted, peeled, and chopped
4 Tbsp (60 mL) olive oil
2 shallots, finely chopped
1 cup (250 mL) chopped fresh cilantro
2 Tbsp (30 mL) lime juice
1 Tbsp (15 mL) lime zest
1½ tsp (7.5 mL) sea salt
1 lb (500 g) halibut fillet
½ tsp (2 mL) freshly ground black pepper
1 ripe tomato, finely chopped
8 soft corn tortillas, warmed
Lime wedges

Roast all the chilies on a gas range or barbecue, or under the broiler, turning them to blacken them on all sides, approximately 10 minutes. Place the blackened peppers in a large bowl and cover with plastic wrap. Allow the peppers to sweat for about 15 minutes until they are cool enough to handle.

Remove the blackened skins and seeds from the peppers, slice them, and place them in a blender. Add the avocado, 3 Tbsp (45 mL) of the olive oil, shallots, cilantro, lime juice, lime zest, and 1 tsp (5 mL) of the salt, and blend until smooth. Add a couple tablespoons of water if the salsa is too thick.

Place a large skillet over medium-high heat and add the remaining 1 Tbsp (15 mL) of olive oil. Season the halibut with the remaining ½ tsp (2 mL) salt and the pepper. Cook the fish about 4 minutes per side or until firm to the touch. Remove the halibut from the pan and cut into small pieces. Divide the tomatoes, salsa, and halibut evenly among the tortillas and serve with lime wedges.

CHICKEN, TURKEY, & DUCK

Serves 4
Prep time: 15 minutes
Cook time: 35 minutes

MOROCCAN CHICKEN

When I was growing up, it was common for me to see cinnamon being used in desserts, but not in main courses. But that was before I went to Morocco and discovered how good cinnamon is in savoury dishes. The harmonious flavours of this dish are North African; the indigenous people in that area have been cooking with these ingredients for centuries. This dish pairs very well with couscous.

CORY'S TIPS

» For a slightly richer flavour, substitute chicken thighs for chicken breasts.

» Using dried apricots instead of cherries will take this dish to yet another level, and apricots are more traditional in Moroccan cuisine.

2 lb (1 kg) boneless, skinless chicken breast
2 tsp (10 mL) hot paprika
1 tsp (5 mL) ground cumin
1 tsp (5 mL) ground cinnamon
1 tsp (5 mL) turmeric
2 Tbsp (30 mL) olive oil
1 shallot, finely chopped
1 Tbsp (15 mL) grated fresh ginger
4 cloves garlic, finely chopped
1 tsp (5 mL) sea salt
1 tsp (5 mL) freshly ground black pepper
½ cup (125 mL) low-sodium vegetable stock
1 cup (250 mL) sliced kalamata olives
½ cup (125 mL) dried cherries
2 Tbsp (30 mL) lemon zest
½ cup (125 mL) chopped fresh parsley

Cut the chicken into bite-sized pieces and combine it with the paprika, cumin, cinnamon, and turmeric in a large bowl. Cover and refrigerate for at least 2 hours or even overnight.

Place a large saucepan over medium-high heat and add the olive oil, shallot, ginger, and garlic. Cook until softened, about 5 minutes. Add the chicken and cook until opaque, about 10 minutes. Season with the salt and pepper. Add the vegetable stock, olives, cherries, and lemon zest. Cover and simmer on medium-low heat for 20 minutes. Garnish each serving with fresh parsley.

Serves 4
Prep time: 20 minutes
Cook time: 25 minutes

SPICY COCONUT CHICKEN IN CURRY SAUCE

This is a variation on the popular "rice bowls" we have become familiar with in restaurants today. I'm a big fan of one-dish meals, as it makes for easy cleanup. Serve this on top of a scoop of brown basmati rice.

CORY'S TIP

» Freeze leftover fresh ginger. It retains a fresh flavour and it is very easy to grate when frozen!

2 lb (1 kg) boneless, skinless chicken breast
1 tsp (5 mL) sea salt
1 tsp (5 mL) freshly ground black pepper
½ tsp (2 mL) ground coriander
½ tsp (2 mL) ground cinnamon
½ tsp (2 mL) ground cloves
¼ tsp (1 mL) turmeric
2 Tbsp (30 mL) olive oil
4 cloves garlic, finely chopped
1 shallot, finely chopped
1 fresh red cayenne chili, seeded and finely chopped
1 Tbsp (15 mL) grated fresh ginger
1 cup (250 mL) light coconut milk
1 tsp (5 mL) cornstarch
¼ cup (60 mL) finely chopped fresh basil

Cut the chicken into bite-sized pieces. Combine the salt, pepper, coriander, cinnamon, cloves, and turmeric in a large bowl and add the chicken. Mix well. Cover and refrigerate for at least 2 hours or even overnight.

Place a large saucepan over medium-high heat and add the olive oil, garlic, and shallot. Cook until softened, about 5 minutes. Add the chili, ginger, and marinated chicken, and cook until the chicken is opaque, about 10 minutes. Reserve 2 Tbsp (30 mL) of the coconut milk, and add the rest to the saucepan. Mix the cornstarch with the reserved coconut milk until it is smooth and free of lumps. Add to the saucepan, stirring until the sauce is thickened. Garnish each serving with the fresh basil.

Serves 4
Prep time: 25 minutes
Cook time: 40 minutes

MANGO CHICKEN IN MADRAS COCONUT CURRY

If you have not yet invited your neighbours for dinner, they may just invite themselves when they smell the delicious aroma of this dish coming from your kitchen. The sweet and savoury combination of mango and curry is hard to beat. The Devil's Eggs (page 16) are a great starter for this delicious curry, which I love to serve with a nutty brown basmati rice.

CORY'S TIPS

» If fresh mangoes are unavailable, you can substitute the canned version, but avoid the ones packed in syrup as they would make the dish too sweet.

» For a different presentation, cook four boneless, skinless chicken breasts in the sauce until cooked through, about 25 to 30 minutes.

2 Tbsp (30 mL) olive oil
1 cup (250 mL) finely chopped shallots
3 cloves garlic, finely chopped
1 red bell pepper, seeded and finely chopped
2 Tbsp (30 mL) grated fresh ginger
2 Tbsp (30 mL) madras curry powder
½ tsp (2 mL) ground cumin
½ tsp (2 mL) ground cayenne
½ tsp (2 mL) ground coriander
1 cup (250 mL) low-sodium vegetable stock
2 mangoes, peeled and finely chopped
2 lb (1 kg) boneless, skinless chicken breast
½ cup (125 mL) yellow raisins
14 oz (398 mL) can light coconut milk
1 tsp (5 mL) sea salt
1 tsp (5 mL) freshly ground black pepper
¼ cup (60 mL) chopped cilantro

Place a large saucepan over medium-high heat and add the olive oil, shallots, garlic, red pepper, ginger, curry powder, cumin, cayenne, and coriander. Cook until softened, about 5 minutes. Stir in the vegetable stock and chopped mango, and bring to a boil. Reduce the heat and simmer for 15 minutes. Using an immersion blender or food processor, blend until smooth and return the puréed sauce to the saucepan.

Cut the chicken into bite-sized pieces and add the chicken and raisins to the saucepan. Cover and simmer for 10 to 15 minutes or until the chicken is cooked (it will turn an opaque white when done). Stir in the coconut milk and season with salt and pepper. Cook an additional 5 minutes on medium-low heat. Garnish with the cilantro.

Serves 4
Prep time: 20 minutes
Cook time: 55 minutes

CORY'S CHICKEN CURRY WITH THAI SPICE

A rich, creamy texture and the sharpness of lemon grass and Greek yogurt are the hallmarks of this dish. Don't be intimidated by the list of ingredients: most Asian food stores carry them. While you're shopping, take the opportunity to browse the specialty items—you may be inspired to create a whole new dish! Serve with basmati rice.

CORY'S TIPS

» Chicken breasts are a healthy choice, although chicken thighs may be used instead.
» If you are unable to find lime leaves, use 1 Tbsp (15 mL) of lime zest.
» Unused lemon grass may be frozen and used at a later date.

2 Tbsp (30 mL) olive oil
3 cloves garlic, finely chopped
1 shallot, finely chopped
2 Tbsp (30 mL) red curry paste
14 oz (398 mL) can light coconut milk
3 cups (750 mL) boiling water
6 lime leaves, chopped
2 stalks lemon grass, roughly chopped
½ cup (125 mL) Greek-style yogurt
2 Tbsp (30 mL) apricot jam
4 boneless, skinless chicken breasts, cubed
1 tsp (5 mL) sea salt
½ tsp (2 mL) freshly ground black pepper
2 Tbsp (30 mL) finely chopped fresh cilantro

Place a medium saucepan over medium-high heat and add the olive oil, garlic, and shallot. Cook until softened, about 5 minutes. Stir in the curry paste, coconut milk, and boiling water. Add the lime leaves, lemon grass, yogurt, and apricot jam, and stir thoroughly. Reduce the heat, cover, and simmer for 30 minutes.

Transfer the sauce to a blender or food processor, and pulse until smooth. Return to the saucepan over medium-high heat and add the chicken. Season with the salt and pepper. Cook until the chicken is opaque, approximately 10 to 15 minutes. Garnish each serving with fresh cilantro. Enjoy!

Serves 4
Prep time: 20 minutes
Cook time: 50 minutes

SWEET & SPICY CHICKEN

This recipe comes to me by way of my family's cookbook. The recipes are rather simple, and that's what I like about them. It doesn't take too much effort or time to make this healthy and flavourful dish, and I don't know anyone who doesn't like sweet and spicy chicken. Serve the chicken over brown rice.

CORY'S TIPS

» You can substitute thigh meat for breast meat for a richer dish.
» If you like your sauce a little thicker, add an extra teaspoon (5 mL) of cornstarch mixed with 2 Tbsp (30 mL) of water. Add to the sauce and simmer to the desired thickness.

4 boneless, skinless chicken breasts
1 Tbsp (15 mL) olive oil
2 cloves garlic, finely chopped
1 Tbsp (15 mL) grated fresh ginger
2 fresh red cayenne chilies, seeded and finely chopped
1 shallot, finely chopped
½ tsp (2 mL) sea salt
½ tsp (2 mL) freshly ground black pepper
14 oz (398 mL) can pineapple chunks
¼ cup (60 mL) light soy sauce
⅓ cup (80 mL) water
¼ cup (60 mL) honey
1 red bell pepper, seeded and finely chopped
14 oz (398 mL) can mushrooms, drained

Cut the chicken into bite-sized pieces. Place a medium saucepan over medium-high heat and add the olive oil. Add the chicken, garlic, ginger, chilies, shallot, salt, and pepper. Cook for about 10 minutes, stirring frequently, until the chicken is opaque. Add the pineapple with its juice, soy sauce, and water, and simmer for 15 minutes. Add the honey and red bell pepper, simmering for an additional 15 minutes. Add the mushrooms, and heat through, about 5 minutes.

Serves 4
Prep time: 20 minutes
Cook time: 50 minutes

CHICKEN SEVILLE

The city of Seville in southern Spain is full of wonderful culinary memories for me, and this dish brings it all back with its fresh flavours and spicy sausage. I made sure to ask for the recipe because I never wanted to forget my experiences. This is great served with any kind of rice, especially the Toasted Pistachio Wild Rice (page 84)!

CORY'S TIPS

» Gently bruise fennel seeds to release their essential oils.

» Nearly any type of sausage can be used here, although my favourite is the traditional chorizo.

2 Tbsp (30 mL) olive oil
4 boneless, skinless chicken breasts, cubed
2 red bell peppers, finely chopped
1 shallot, finely chopped
½ cup (125 mL) finely chopped spicy sausage
2 cloves garlic, finely chopped
28 oz (796 mL) can diced tomatoes
1 tsp (5 mL) sea salt
1 tsp (5 mL) freshly ground black pepper
¼ tsp (1 mL) fennel seeds
¼ tsp (1 mL) fresh marjoram leaves
¼ tsp (1 mL) chopped fresh thyme leaves
4 whole sprigs fresh flat-leaf parsley

Place a large skillet over medium-high heat and add 1 Tbsp (15 mL) of the olive oil. Brown the chicken in the olive oil for about 10 minutes. Remove from the pan and set aside. Add the remaining 1 Tbsp (15 mL) olive oil to the pan and cook the bell peppers, shallot, sausage, and garlic until tender, about 5 minutes. Return the browned chicken to the pan, add the tomatoes, and stir in the salt, pepper, fennel seeds, marjoram, and thyme. Bring to a boil. Reduce the heat to a simmer, cover, and cook for 20 minutes. Garnish each serving with a sprig of parsley.

Serves 4 to 6
Prep time: 25 minutes
Cook time: 40 minutes

CHICKEN JAMBALAYA

Another meal in a bowl, this dish is particularly hearty, comprising both chicken and chorizo. This dish freezes very well. I like making large batches of it with the fresh herbs, chilies, and tomatoes from my organic garden and freezing them in serving sizes so I can enjoy the taste of summer when winter arrives.

CORY'S TIPS

» For a richer dish, substitute the dark meat of chicken thighs for breast meat.

» If you prefer to use fresh basil and thyme, simply substitute 1 tsp (5 mL) fresh for ½ tsp (2 mL) dried herbs.

» You may use raw chorizo instead of cured, but be sure to remove it from its casing. Cook it separately first; then drain and set aside. Add to the saucepan with the chicken.

1 Tbsp (15 mL) olive oil
1¼ cups (310 mL) brown or basmati rice
1¼ cups (310 mL) finely chopped celery
1 cup (250 mL) finely chopped red bell pepper
½ cup (125 mL) finely chopped shallots
1 clove garlic, finely chopped
2½ lb (1.25 kg) finely chopped cured chorizo sausage
½ tsp (2 mL) ground cayenne
½ tsp (2 mL) ground cumin
½ tsp (2 mL) dried basil
½ tsp (2 mL) dried thyme
½ tsp (2 mL) hot paprika
½ tsp (2 mL) freshly ground black pepper
1 bay leaf
1 cup (250 mL) chopped tomatoes
½ cup (125 mL) tomato juice
½ cup (125 mL) low-sodium chicken stock
½ lb (250 g) boneless, skinless chicken breast, cubed

Place a large saucepan over medium-high heat and add the oil and rice. Cook until the rice is golden, about 5 minutes. Add the celery, bell pepper, shallots, and garlic. Cook until softened, about 5 minutes. Add the sausage, cayenne, cumin, basil, thyme, paprika, pepper, and bay leaf, mixing thoroughly. Stir in the tomatoes, tomato juice, and chicken stock. Simmer for 10 minutes.

Add the chicken to the saucepan and bring to a boil. Reduce the heat, cover, and simmer until the rice is tender and the liquid has been absorbed, about 15 minutes. Let stand for 10 minutes. Remove the bay leaf before serving.

Serves 4 to 6
Prep time: 20 minutes
Cook time: 1¾ hours

ROAST CHICKEN WITH HARISSA STUFFING (MOROCCAN STYLE!)

This dish is a step up from everyday roast chicken, which makes for a refreshing change. I have even made it for Christmas dinner. In summer my cherry tree produces an abundance of beautiful, sweet red organic cherries, which I dry and incorporate into this dish, along with the traditional apricots and raisins. The touch of cinnamon is traditionally Moroccan, and the recipe is a perfect balance of sweet and savoury—though I cannot resist adding a few of my fresh cayenne chilies from the garden! Spicy Sweet Potatoes with Fresh Ginger (page 88) are an excellent accompaniment for this dish.

CORY'S TIPS

» If you forget to soak the fruits overnight, an hour in hot water will be sufficient to soften them.

» Raisins and apricots are the usual fruits used in this dish, but nothing is written in stone, so experiment with your favourite dried fruits and create your own trip to Morocco!

» Harissa is a very hot North African spice blend made from hot chilies, tomatoes, and paprika. I buy my harissa spice as a paste; it is readily available in the import section of most grocers.

2 Tbsp (30 mL) butter
2 cloves garlic, finely chopped
1 shallot, finely chopped
2 tsp (10 mL) ground cinnamon
1 tsp (5 mL) ground cumin
½ cup (125 mL) chopped toasted almonds
1 cup (250 mL) dried fruits, soaked overnight, drained, and roughly chopped
1 tsp (5 mL) sea salt
½ tsp (2 mL) freshly ground black pepper
1 whole chicken, about 3 to 4 lb (1.5 kg to 1.8 kg)
2 bay leaves
2 tsp (10 mL) honey
2 tsp (10 mL) tomato paste
¼ cup (60 mL) lemon juice
½ cup (125 mL) low-sodium chicken stock
1 tsp (5 mL) harissa spice

Preheat the oven to 400°F (200°C). Place a medium saucepan over medium-high heat and add the butter, garlic, and shallot. Cook until softened, about 5 minutes. Stir in the cinnamon and cumin, and continue cooking for 2 minutes. Add the almonds and rehydrated fruit. Season with the salt and pepper.

Place the chicken in a roasting pan. Stuff the chicken with the fruit and nut mixture. Tuck in the bay leaves and roast for 1½ hours, basting occasionally, until the juices run clear and a thermometer inserted in the centre of the chicken registers 180°F (82°C). Remove the chicken from the roasting pan and tent loosely with foil.

Stir the honey, tomato paste, lemon juice, chicken stock, and harissa into the pan juices and bring to a boil. Reduce the heat to low and simmer for 2 minutes. Transfer the stuffing to a serving bowl and remove the bay leaves. Carve the chicken and pour sauce over each serving. Serve the stuffing on the side.

Serves 4
Prep time: 20 minutes
Cook time: 30 minutes

SPICY CHICKEN WITH CHILI-GARLIC MARINADE

I love to make this dish during the late summer months and set a gorgeous table on the patio. I use fresh chilies from my garden; the heat from the fresh chilies and the savoury flavours will keep you warm and satisfied on cooler summer nights. The fresh taste and crisp texture of my Fennel-Apple Salad (page 49) pairs beautifully with this dish.

CORY'S TIPS

» For best results, marinate chicken overnight in the refrigerator.
» It's important to bring the chicken to room temperature before broiling it, as the sudden temperature change can "shock" the meat and cause it to become tight and tough.
» Honey may be used in place of the brown sugar, or raw cane sugar, which adds a wonderful flavour.

1 cup (250 mL) toasted cashews
5 Tbsp (75 mL) roughly chopped cilantro
4 cloves garlic, roughly chopped
2 Tbsp (30 mL) olive oil
1 Tbsp (15 mL) light soy sauce
2 fresh red cayenne chilies, seeded and roughly chopped
2 Tbsp (30 mL) lime juice
2 tsp (10 mL) brown sugar
½ tsp (2 mL) sea salt
½ tsp (2 mL) freshly ground black pepper
12 boneless, skinless chicken thighs
Lime wedges

In a food processor or blender, combine the cashews, 4 Tbsp (60 mL) of the cilantro, garlic, olive oil, soy sauce, chilies, lime juice, and brown sugar. Blend until smooth. Season with the salt and pepper. Reserve one-quarter of the marinade and place the rest in a medium bowl. Add the chicken and turn to coat evenly in the marinade. Cover and refrigerate for at least 2 hours or overnight. Remove from the refrigerator 20 minutes before cooking.

Preheat the broiler in your oven. Place the chicken thighs on a large, non-stick, rimmed cooking sheet and place on the top rack of the oven. Cook for 25 to 30 minutes, turning frequently, and basting with the reserved marinade every 10 minutes. The chicken is done when a meat thermometer registers 175°F (80°C) and the chicken appears golden brown. Garnish with lime wedges and the remaining 1 Tbsp (15 mL) cilantro.

Serves 4
Prep time: 20 minutes
Cook time: 25 minutes

CHILI-FRIED CHICKEN

Most of us would like to be a little healthier when it comes to what we eat, but busy lives sometimes make that difficult. This protein-rich recipe offers a lot of fresh flavour in a short time for when you are on the go—and it's conveniently all in one dish!

CORY'S TIPS

» Feel free to use other Asian sauces instead of the soy sauce.
» For an interesting change, substitute boiled soba noodles for the brown rice.

4 boneless, skinless chicken breasts
2 Tbsp (30 mL) olive oil
1 cup (250 mL) finely chopped celery
1 red bell pepper, finely chopped
1 Tbsp (15 mL) grated fresh ginger
1 shallot, finely chopped
1 tsp (5 mL) sea salt
1 cup (250 mL) fresh bean sprouts
2 fresh red cayenne chilies, seeded and finely chopped
5 oz (150 g) can water chestnuts, sliced
1 cup (250 mL) low-sodium chicken stock
2 tsp (10 mL) cornstarch
2 Tbsp (30 mL) light soy sauce
3 cups (750 mL) cooked brown rice
¾ cup (185 mL) toasted cashews

Cut the chicken into ¼-inch (0.5 cm) strips. Place a large skillet over medium-high heat and add 1 Tbsp (15 mL) of the olive oil, the celery, red pepper, ginger, shallot, and salt. Cook until softened, about 5 minutes. Remove the vegetables and set aside.

Heat the remaining 1 Tbsp (15 mL) olive oil in the pan, add the chicken, and stir-fry until it is opaque, about 10 minutes. Return the vegetables to the pan. Add the sprouts, chilies, water chestnuts, and chicken stock. Blend the cornstarch with the soy sauce in a small bowl. Add to the pan, stirring and simmering for 5 minutes or until the sauce reaches the desired thickness. Serve over rice, and garnish with the toasted cashews.

Serves 6
Prep time: 20 minutes
Cook time: 1¼ hours

TENDER TURKEY CHILI

Turkey is satisfying without being too heavy or high in fat. I have made a very large batch of this chili and frozen it in meal-sized containers for those nights when it seems there just isn't enough time to cook dinner.

CORY'S TIPS

» Turkey is a healthy choice, but you may use any cooked ground meat. I have used both cooked ground venison and moose.
» If you like, add a garnish of shredded cheddar cheese or sour cream.
» Experiment with other beans, such as black beans and chickpeas.
» Adding puréed roasted vegetables is a great way to fortify this turkey chili to ensure you're getting enough vegetables (and no one will know if you don't tell them!).

2 Tbsp (30 mL) olive oil
2 cups (500 mL) finely chopped shallots
1 cup (250 mL) finely chopped red bell pepper
4 cloves garlic, finely chopped
1 Tbsp (15 mL) ground cumin
1 Tbsp (15 mL) red pepper flakes
2 Tbsp (30 mL) chili powder
3 lb (1.5 kg) ground turkey
Two 28 oz (796 mL) cans crushed tomatoes
2 Tbsp (30 mL) tomato paste
¾ cup (185 mL) low-sodium chicken stock
Two 19 oz (540 mL) cans kidney beans, drained
1 tsp (5 mL) dried oregano
1 Tbsp (10 mL) sea salt
1 tsp (5 mL) freshly ground black pepper

Place a large stockpot over medium-high heat and add the olive oil, shallots, red bell pepper, and garlic. Cook until softened, about 5 minutes. Add the cumin, red pepper flakes, and chili powder, stirring continuously for about 3 minutes. Add the ground turkey, and brown for 10 minutes. Add the tomatoes, tomato paste, chicken stock, beans, oregano, salt, and pepper. Simmer uncovered for 1 hour.

Serves 4
Prep time: 15 minutes
Cook time: 40 minutes

DUCK WITH GREEN APPLES & CHERRY BALSAMIC SAUCE

If you get tired of having the usual beef, pork, chicken, or fish over and over, why not try duck? This succulent meat stands up very well to strong flavours. I recommend you try this recipe if you find yourself in the cooking doldrums. You'll be sure to be re-inspired—the sauce is to die for! Both red and white wines work well with this dish, although I prefer a full-bodied deep red.

CORY'S TIP
» Pat the duck dry with paper towels because dry meat sears better.

4 boneless duck breasts
2 Tbsp (30 mL) butter
3 shallots, finely chopped
2 cloves garlic, finely chopped
3 Granny Smith apples, cored and thinly sliced
1½ cups (375 mL) dried cherries
1 cup (250 mL) balsamic vinegar
1 cup (250 mL) apple cider
½ cup (125 mL) maple syrup

Preheat the oven to 425°F (220°C). Score the duck breast on the fatty side in a cross-hatch pattern. Place a medium saucepan over medium-high heat. Cook the duck, fat side down, until browned, about 5 minutes. Transfer the duck to a large, rimmed baking sheet (fat side up) and bake on the centre rack of the oven for 15 to 20 minutes, or until a thermometer inserted in the duck reaches 180°F (82°C).

Place a medium saucepan over medium-high heat and add the butter, shallots, and garlic. Cook until softened, about 5 minutes. Add the apples, cherries, balsamic vinegar, apple cider, and maple syrup. Cook until the liquid is reduced by one-half. Slice the duck breast thickly across the grain as this will provide a greater surface area, and dress with the cherry balsamic sauce for the perfect presentation!

BEEF, PORK, & LAMB

Serves 4
Prep time: 10 minutes
Cook time: 20 minutes

BARBECUED TENDERLOIN STEAK WITH CRIMINI–BLUE CHEESE SAUCE

When shooting this dish, my photographer couldn't stop drooling! The blue cheese pairs perfectly with the earthy flavour of the mushrooms. This is a feast your guests will never forget! Experiment with different cheeses, and create your own signature steak and mushroom dinner. Try serving it with my delicious New Potatoes with Garden-Fresh Herb Vinaigrette (page 90).

CORY'S TIPS

» Any tender cut of steak can be used instead of tenderloin.
» I've substituted brie for the blue cheese with exceptional results; an in-between option is a cross between blue and brie known as Cambozola. It is creamy, and it has a not-too-overpowering hint of blue cheese.
» Fresh chanterelle mushrooms, when they are in season, are an excellent substitute for the crimini.

Four 6 oz (175 g) thick-cut tenderloin steaks
2 tsp (10 mL) sea salt
2 tsp (10 mL) freshly ground black pepper
1 Tbsp (15 mL) butter
1 lb (500 g) sliced crimini mushrooms
½ cup (125 mL) crumbled blue cheese
2 tsp (10 mL) chopped fresh thyme leaves (or 1 tsp/2 mL dried)

Preheat the barbecue to 400°F (200°C). Season the steaks with 1 tsp (5 mL) of the salt and 1 tsp (5 mL) of the pepper. Place on the grill and cook to your desired level of doneness. (I prefer my steak rare to medium-rare, especially the tenderloin, as it has a tendency to dry out.) Remove the steaks from the heat, tent loosely with foil, and let rest for 5 minutes.

Place a medium saucepan over medium-high heat and add the butter and sliced mushrooms. Season with the remaining 1 tsp (5 mL) salt and pepper. Cook the mushrooms for 5 minutes. Reduce the heat to low and add the blue cheese and thyme. Heat for an additional 5 minutes before serving over the barbecued steaks.

Serves 4
Prep time: 15 minutes
Cook time: 15 minutes

PARSONS RANCH SUNDAY BRUNCH EGGS BENNY

If you ever wake up on a Sunday morning and wonder *What should I make for breakfast?* this recipe is a sure winner. There are a number of options for keeping it interesting, including smoked salmon, lox, baby shrimp, hollandaise sauce, or the Béarnaise sauce here.

CORY'S TIPS

» If you do not have access to farm-fresh eggs, look in your grocery case for free-run (or free-range) eggs, as these are about as close as you're going to get. The difference in taste and colour is noticeable and well worth the extra money.

» Be sure to keep your poaching water at a very light boil—this will help keep the egg whites from separating from the yolks.

8 cups (2 L) water
2 tsp (10 mL) sea salt
6 farm-fresh eggs (see Tips)
2 English muffins, halved
4 slices honey ham
3 Tbsp (45 mL) lemon juice
⅓ cup (80 mL) butter
1 Tbsp (15 mL) finely chopped shallot
1 tsp (5 mL) freshly ground black pepper
1 tsp (5 mL) fresh tarragon, chopped
2 Tbsp (30 mL) white wine
¼ cup (60 mL) finely chopped chives

Place a large deep saucepan over medium-high heat and bring the water to a low boil. Season with the salt. Crack four of the eggs carefully into the water, and cook until soft-poached, about 5 minutes.

Meanwhile, place the English muffins on a baking sheet and broil until the muffins are toasted, about 3 minutes. Remove from the oven and place one slice of ham on each half. Top with the poached eggs.

To make the Béarnaise sauce, separate the remaining two eggs and discard the whites. Place a medium saucepan over low heat and whisk the egg yolks and lemon juice until combined. Whisk in half the butter and the shallot, pepper, tarragon, and wine. Cook until the shallots are soft, about 5 minutes, then add the rest of the butter and whisk briskly until fully combined. Pour the sauce over the poached eggs and garnish with chives.

Serves 4
Prep time: 15 minutes
Cook time: 40 minutes

PAPRIKA PORK CHOPS WITH FRESH FENNEL SEEDS

Sweet and savoury fennel and pork are a wonderful match. Once you have tried this dish, you'll forget forever the dried-out pork chops your mom used to make. Pork has long been considered the other white meat and is a very healthy protein, provided you trim away most of the fat. It pairs well with white wine and, in this instance, is equal to a full-bodied red. This is delicious with either basmati rice or pasta.

CORY'S TIPS

» If you don't have access to fresh fennel seeds, the same amount of the dried seeds will work just fine.
» Ask your butcher to cut your pork chops extra thick, which helps to keep them from drying out during cooking.
» When browning meat, place it in the pan and don't move it about, to give it a seared, caramelized finish. You'll know it's ready when it comes away from the pan easily and is a golden brown colour.

1 Tbsp (15 mL) olive oil
4 pork chop steaks
2 shallots, finely chopped
2 tsp (10 mL) fresh fennel seeds, lightly crushed
1 Tbsp (15 mL) hot paprika
14 oz (398 mL) can diced tomatoes
½ tsp (2 mL) sea salt
½ tsp (2 mL) freshly ground black pepper
2 Tbsp (30 mL) sour cream

Place a large saucepan over medium-high heat and add the olive oil. Brown the pork chops on both sides, about 3 minutes per side. Remove from the heat, tent loosely with foil, and set aside.

Add the shallots to the saucepan and cook until softened, about 5 minutes. Stir in the fennel, paprika, and tomatoes. Return the pork chops to the saucepan, reduce the heat, and simmer very gently for 30 minutes or until cooked through. Season with the salt and pepper. Swirl in the sour cream just before serving.

Serves 4 to 6
Prep time: 35 minutes
Cook time: 1¾ hours

CORY'S CAYENNE CHILI WITH RUSTIC CORNBREAD

This dish takes a little bit of work but if you love fiery food, it will all be worth it. The recipe came to me from a friend who is a fireman and used to drink hot sauce by the bottle. My cayenne chili is not that hot, but it's definitely a three-alarm dish. I like to use stout or porter in the dish because of its rich flavour and hoppy aroma.

CORY'S TIPS

» For a milder version, try this recipe using half the chilies and work your way up.
» If you'd like to fortify your chili with more vegetables, add roasted and puréed sweet potatoes, carrots, or zucchini. Your kids will eat their vegetables and not even know it! (Though you may have to adjust the spice to their taste.)
» Again, wear rubber gloves when you seed and chop the chilies.

½ lb (250 g) smoked bacon, finely chopped
1 lb (500 g) fresh ground beef
1 lb (500 g) fresh ground pork
6 jalapeño chilies, seeded and finely chopped
6 fresh cayenne chilies, seeded and finely chopped
6 ancho chilies, seeded and finely chopped
4 cloves garlic, finely chopped
2 shallots, finely chopped
1 red bell pepper, seeded and finely chopped
2 Tbsp (30 mL) chili powder
1½ Tbsp (22.5 mL) ground cumin
1 Tbsp (15 mL) red pepper flakes
28 oz (796 mL) can crushed tomatoes
28 oz (796 mL) can diced tomatoes, drained
1 Tbsp (15 mL) tomato paste
12 oz (355 mL) bottle dark beer
2 cups (500 mL) low-sodium chicken stock
19 oz (540 mL) can black beans, drained and rinsed
19 oz (540 mL) can kidney beans, drained and rinsed
19 oz (540 mL) can chickpeas, drained and rinsed

Place a large stockpot over medium-high heat and add the bacon. Cook until browned, about 5 minutes. Add the beef and pork, and cook, stirring frequently, until the meat is evenly browned, about 15 minutes. Stir in the jalapeño, cayenne, and ancho chilies, garlic, shallots, bell pepper, chili powder, cumin, and red pepper flakes. Add the crushed and diced tomatoes, tomato paste, beer, and chicken stock, and stir well. Reduce the heat to low and simmer for 45 minutes.

Add beans and chickpeas and continue simmering for 30 minutes longer. Serve with the cornbread (page 140).

Makes one loaf
Prep time: 10 minutes
Cook time: 35 minutes

RUSTIC CORNBREAD

Not only is this rustic cornbread perfect with my cayenne chili, it's also wonderful with ribs and chicken. I even love to serve it with Christmas dinner.

CORY'S TIPS

» For an exciting twist, substitute a large chipotle chili in adobo sauce for the chilies.

» For a slightly smoother texture, use finely ground cornmeal instead of medium- or coarse-ground.

» To raise the nutrition quotient, try using whole wheat or multigrain flour instead of the all-purpose flour.

2 large eggs
2 cups (500 mL) buttermilk
¼ cup (60 mL) butter, melted
½ cup (125 mL) all-purpose flour
1 tsp (5 mL) baking soda
1 tsp (5 mL) sea salt
¼ tsp (1 mL) ground mace
2½ cups (625 mL) medium-grind cornmeal
2 fresh cayenne chilies, seeded and finely chopped

Preheat the oven to 400°F (200°C). Grease a 9- × 5-inch (2 L) loaf pan and flour lightly. Whisk the eggs, buttermilk, and melted butter in a large bowl until frothy. Combine the flour, baking soda, salt, and mace, and sift into the bowl. Gradually fold in the cornmeal, a little at a time. Stir in the fresh chilies and pour the mixture into the prepared pan.

Bake on the centre rack for 25 to 30 minutes or until the top is firm to the touch. Remove from the oven and allow the loaf to cool for 5 minutes before turning out. Sprinkle lightly with Himalayan pink salt or *fleur de sel* and serve warm.

Serves 4 to 6
Prep time: 15 minutes
Cook time: 1¼ hours

FIERY BOURBON-BAKED MAPLE RIBS

It's paramount to use real maple syrup in this recipe as "maple-flavoured syrup" is not what we're looking for! This recipe has been a closely guarded family secret, until now. (Now you can keep it in your family!) I enjoy a little bit of Jack Daniel's in my ribs—and for the cook, Jack Daniel's with a little cola and lime.

CORY'S TIPS

» I like to trim away as much fat as possible, as these ribs are already full of flavour and always tender.

» Don't forget to remove that membrane, or silver skin, on the back of the ribs with a sharp knife. Ask your butcher to trim the ribs for you to speed up the preparation process.

2 Tbsp (30 mL) olive oil
2 cloves garlic, finely chopped
1 shallot, thinly sliced
1 Tbsp (15 mL) red wine vinegar
1 tsp (5 mL) ground cayenne
1 tsp (5 mL) prepared horseradish
1 tsp (5 mL) hot paprika
1 tsp (5 mL) grated fresh ginger
1 Tbsp (15 mL) ketchup
1 Tbsp (15 mL) Worcestershire sauce
1 Tbsp (15 mL) light soy sauce
½ cup (125 mL) maple syrup
¼ cup (60 mL) bourbon
2½ lb (1.25 kg) pork spare ribs, fat trimmed

Preheat the oven to 400°F (200°C). Place a medium saucepan on medium-high heat and add the olive oil, garlic, and shallot. Cook until softened, about 5 minutes. Add the vinegar, cayenne, horseradish, paprika, ginger, ketchup, Worcestershire sauce, soy sauce, maple syrup, and bourbon, and bring to a boil. Lower the heat to a simmer and cook for 5 minutes.

Place the ribs in a single layer in a large roasting pan and pour the sauce over the ribs, coating them thoroughly. Cover the pan with foil and bake for 45 minutes. Remove the foil and bake an additional 20 minutes, basting frequently. The ribs will be sticky so be sure to have plenty of napkins on hand.

Serves 4
Prep time: 20 minutes
Cook time: 2 hours

TENDER BABY BACK RIBS WITH FIERY COLA SAUCE

Well, let it be said that if you like messy ribs you'll absolutely love these guys! I have never had any leftovers and once you taste them, you'll know why. The ribs are so tender and juicy, the meat falls right off the bone! I love to serve these with a cold beer or a full-bodied red wine. Oh, and you'd better have tons of paper towels on hand, too, because these are meant to be picked up and devoured! You will need 2 cups (500 mL) of hickory chips for these ribs; soak the chips in water for one hour.

CORY'S TIPS

» Remember to remove the silver skin (membrane) from the underside of the rack of ribs, as it will remain tough (or ask your butcher to do it when you buy the ribs).

» These ribs may be made in the oven as well, but you'll want to omit the smoke pouch. Cook for the same length of time at 325°F (160°C).

RIBS

1 clove garlic, finely chopped
1 Tbsp (15 mL) ground cayenne
2 tsp (10 mL) sea salt
1 tsp (5 mL) freshly ground black pepper
2½ lb (1.25 kg) baby back ribs

FIERY COLA SAUCE

1 Tbsp (15 mL) olive oil
½ tsp (2 mL) finely chopped fresh garlic
1 tsp (5 mL) ground cayenne
½ tsp (2 mL) ground cumin
½ cup (125 mL) ketchup
½ cup (125 mL) cola-flavoured carbonated drink
2 Tbsp (30 mL) cider vinegar
½ tsp (2 mL) freshly ground black pepper

To make the dry rub for the ribs, combine the garlic, cayenne, salt, and pepper in a small bowl. Rub the mixture all over the ribs, pressing firmly.

Using a propane grill, place the chips in a foil pouch, perforate the pouch with a fork to allow smoke to escape, and place directly on the gas burner. When the grill temperature is about 300°F (150°C), place the ribs on the grill over indirect heat, and cook until they're very tender and the meat comes away from the bone easily, 1½ to 2 hours.

While the ribs are grilling, make the sauce. Place a medium saucepan over medium-high heat and add the olive oil, garlic, cayenne, and cumin, stirring occasionally. Cook until the garlic is soft, about 5 minutes. Add the remaining ingredients and simmer for 10 minutes.

Approximately 25 minutes before the ribs are done, brush the sauce on both sides of the ribs, turning every 5 minutes. Remove the ribs from the grill, tent loosely with foil, and let rest for 10 minutes before serving.

Serves 4 to 6
Prep time: 30 minutes
Cook time: 2½ hours

CHOCOLATE & COFFEE BRAISED RIBS

This recipe will make you new friends, and make your old friends like you even more. Be sure to have lots of paper towels on hand, as these ribs get messy, but I guarantee no one will be complaining. If you've ever tried chili and chocolate together, you will know how well this combination works. I like to serve these with a nice cold beer with a wedge of lime.

CORY'S TIPS

» Use the darkest coffee roast possible, or even espresso, for full flavour.
» Raw cane sugar is sometimes called turbinado-style sugar.
» The membrane, or silver skin, on the back of the ribs should be removed before cooking, as it remains tough. You can do this yourself with a sharp-tipped knife, or ask your butcher to do it for you when you buy the ribs.

5 lb (2.2 kg) beef short ribs
1 Tbsp (15 mL) sea salt
2 tsp (10 mL) freshly ground black pepper
¼ cup (60 mL) olive oil
2 shallots, finely chopped
1 jalepeño pepper, seeded and finely chopped
1 red bell pepper, seeded and finely chopped
4 cloves garlic, finely chopped
2 Tbsp (30 mL) raw cane sugar
2 Tbsp (30 mL) ancho chili powder
¼ cup (60 mL) chopped fresh oregano
1 tsp (5 mL) ground cumin
1 Tbsp (15 mL) tomato paste
28 oz (796 mL) can diced tomatoes
2 cups (500 mL) freshly brewed strong coffee
1 cup (250 mL) chopped dark chocolate
   (75% cocoa)

Preheat the oven to 300°F (150°C). Sprinkle the ribs with the salt and pepper, and rub it in thoroughly. Place a large ovenproof saucepan over medium-high heat and add the olive oil. Working in small batches, sear the ribs in the oil until browned, about 5 minutes per side. Set the ribs aside.

Reduce the heat to medium and add the shallots and jalapeño and bell pepper. Cook until softened, about 5 minutes. Add the garlic, cane sugar, chili powder, oregano, and cumin, and cook for 5 minutes. Stir in the tomato paste, tomatoes, and coffee, and bring to a boil. Add the seared ribs to the pan and return to a boil.

Cover and bake in the preheated oven for approximately 2 hours. Remove from the oven and stir in the chocolate until well incorporated.

Serves 4
Prep time: 20 minutes
Cook time: 45 minutes

CINNAMON-CRUSTED RACK OF LAMB

I am often asked to make this dish for special occasions and I'm always eager to do so. Lamb is one of my favourite meats, and this dish showcases just how good it can be. "Frenched" just means that the meat has been trimmed away from the upper end of the bones to give it a neat appearance. I like to introduce this dish as "lambsicles" because the bones are like Popsicle sticks.

CORY'S TIP
» Ask your butcher to french your rack of lamb for you. It's not mandatory for this recipe but it does make the presentation a little cleaner, and the bare bones look beautiful roasted.

1 cup (250 mL) panko (Japanese breadcrumbs)
1 Tbsp (15 mL) preserved green peppercorns, drained
1 Tbsp (15 mL) ground cinnamon
2 cloves garlic, finely chopped
½ tsp (2 mL) sea salt
½ tsp (2 mL) freshly ground black pepper
2 Tbsp (30 mL) butter, melted
4 racks of lamb, frenched, each with 4 bones
2 tsp (10 mL) Dijon or grainy mustard
1½ cups (375 mL) low-sodium chicken stock
¼ cup (60 mL) red wine
1 Tbsp (15 mL) balsamic vinegar

Preheat the oven to 425°F (220°C). Spread the panko on a large, rimmed baking sheet and toast until golden, about 5 minutes.

In a medium bowl, combine the panko, peppercorns, cinnamon, garlic, salt, pepper, and melted butter. Mix thoroughly. Coat the racks with the mustard and then press the panko mixture on evenly to form a crust. Place the racks in a roasting pan and roast for 25 to 30 minutes for medium-rare. Remove the lamb to a cutting board, tent loosely with foil, and allow to rest.

Place the roasting pan over medium-high heat and stir the stock, wine, and balsamic vinegar into the juices in the pan. Bring to a boil. Lower the heat and simmer until reduced to a rich gravy that will coat the back of a spoon, about 10 minutes. Carve the lamb and serve with the gravy on the side.

Serves 4
Prep time: 25 minutes
Cook time: 2 hours

BRAISED LAMB CHOPS WITH SPICY CURRY SAUCE

This recipe was inspired by a meal I had in a little restaurant in southern England. It was a rainy late night in October, and I was cold and hungry. The restaurant owner was just closing up and saw me looking in the window. He took pity and offered me a table inside. Little did I know that on that rainy night I would have the best lamb dish of my entire life. I encourage you to try this one and find out if it is your #1 too! Serve with seasonal vegetables and basmati rice, and enjoy.

CORY'S TIP
» If lamb chops are not available, you can substitute any cut of lamb.

3 Tbsp (45 mL) Dijon mustard
2 Tbsp (30 mL) hot paprika
2 Tbsp (30 mL) medium curry powder
1 tsp (5 mL) ground coriander
1 tsp (5 mL) freshly ground black pepper
1 fresh red cayenne chili, seeded and finely chopped
8 lamb chops
2 Tbsp (30 mL) olive oil
5 cloves garlic, finely chopped
1 shallot, finely chopped
1 tsp (5 mL) sea salt

In a medium mixing bowl, combine the mustard, paprika, curry powder, coriander, pepper, and chili. Mix well. Add the lamb chops and coat completely with the mixture. Cover and refrigerate for a couple of hours or up to overnight.

Preheat the oven to 300°F (150°C). Place a large ovenproof skillet over medium-high heat and add the olive oil, garlic, and shallot. Cook until softened, about 5 minutes. Season the chops with the salt and brown on both sides, about 3 minutes per side. Place the pan in the preheated oven and cook for 1½ hours.

Serves 4
Prep time: 20 minutes
Cook time: 2 to 3 hours

SPRING LAMB STEW

Some days I don't feel like spending my time working in the kitchen, so on those days I bring out my large stockpot and let it do the work for me. I can tell you from experience that the aroma of this dish simmering on the stove is a little slice of heaven. This recipe was made for slow cooking! Low and slow means tender and juicy.

CORY'S TIPS

» Rosemary and garlic pair very well with lamb, so don't be afraid to be generous.

» Any cut of lamb may be used here, although I find the shoulder and leg portions work the best.

4 lb (1.8 kg) spring lamb, cubed
5 cloves garlic, finely chopped
1 Tbsp (15 mL) finely chopped fresh rosemary
1 cup (250 mL) dry red wine
2 Tbsp (30 mL) olive oil
1 shallot, finely chopped
1 tsp (5 mL) sea salt
1 tsp (5 mL) freshly ground black pepper
2 cups (500 mL) roasted red bell peppers,
    drained and sliced
1 Tbsp (15 mL) sweet hot paprika
¼ cup (60 mL) chopped fresh parsley
½ cup (125 mL) low-sodium vegetable stock

In a large mixing bowl combine the lamb, garlic, rosemary, and ½ cup (125 mL) of the red wine. Cover and refrigerate for 3 hours.

Place a large saucepan over medium-high heat and add the olive oil, shallot, and lamb. Discard the marinade. Brown the lamb on all sides, about 15 minutes. Season with salt and pepper. Stir in the roasted peppers, paprika, parsley, and the remaining ½ cup (125 mL) red wine, and bring to a boil. Reduce the heat and simmer for about 15 minutes or until the juice has thickened slightly. Stir in the vegetable stock, cover, and simmer on the lowest heat for 2 to 2½ hours or until the meat is very tender.

DELECTABLES

Serves 4
Prep time: 10 minutes
Cook time: 20 minutes

CARIBBEAN BANANAS FLAMBÉ

My first experience with this dish was on a cruise ship when I was only 15 years old. I thought it was an amazing spectacle, and loved all the excitement of setting something on fire and then eating it! (The fact that I got to have a little bit of rum was good, too.) This dish is fun at a party. Remember to dim the lights to spotlight your dramatic presentation.

CORY'S TIPS

» I recommend Appleton Estate rum, but you can use any dark rum of your choice.
» Raw cane sugar is sometimes called turbinado-style sugar.
» It is always a good idea when setting things alight indoors to keep a damp tea towel handy to blanket any excessive flames, should the need arise.

4 firm ripe bananas, peeled and cut lengthwise
2 Tbsp (30 mL) lime juice
½ cup (125 mL) raw cane sugar
1 tsp (5 mL) ground allspice
1 Tbsp (15 mL) grated fresh ginger
6 cardamom pods, seeds removed and crushed
2 Tbsp (30 mL) butter
¼ cup (60 mL) dark rum
2 cups (500 mL) vanilla ice cream

Preheat the oven to 400°F (200°C). Place the bananas in a single layer in a 9-inch (2.5 L) square baking dish. Drizzle with the lime juice.

In a medium bowl, combine the sugar, allspice, ginger, and cardamom. Sprinkle evenly over the bananas. Dot with the butter and bake for 15 minutes or until the bananas are soft. Remove from the oven and set on a serving table.

Place a small saucepan over low heat and warm the rum for about 3 minutes. Pour over the bananas and carefully set it alight! When the flames are gone, top each serving with ½ cup (125 mL) of vanilla ice cream.

Serves 6
Prep time: 10 minutes
Cook time: 30 minutes

CORY'S CINNAMON APPLE BERRY CRISP

This is very simple to make, and the steel-cut oats contribute vitamin B and fibre. Use this recipe as a guideline: I throw in whatever fruits I have on hand, which gives the dessert its own unique flavour every time. There are no limits to the fruit combinations you can make! For an added bonus, serve this with vanilla ice cream.

CORY'S TIP

» Steel-cut oats are coarsely cut oats, as opposed to the flatter rolled oats. I've found that they make the best crust in this dessert, although large-flake rolled oats will also work.

5 cups (1.25 L) peeled and sliced apples
2 cups (500 mL) mixed berries
⅓ cup (80 mL) water
1 cup (250 mL) all-purpose flour
¾ cup (185 mL) brown sugar
½ cup (125 mL) steel-cut oats
½ tsp (2 mL) ground cinnamon
½ tsp (2 mL) sea salt
½ cup (125 mL) butter, melted

Preheat the oven to 350°F (180°C). Butter a 9- × 5-inch (2 L) loaf pan. Spread the apples in the pan and top with the mixed berries. Sprinkle with the water.

Combine the flour, sugar, oats, cinnamon, and salt in a medium bowl. Add the melted butter, and mix well to form a crumbly texture. Spread evenly over the fruit. Bake in the centre of the oven for 30 minutes, or until the topping is browned and the apples are tender. Remove from the oven and let stand for 10 minutes before serving.

Serves 6
Prep time: 20 minutes
Cook time: 30 minutes

RICH DARK CHOCOLATE POACHED PEARS

This favourite is a special occasion dessert that is well worth the extra time and effort. Make this when you're trying to impress a new lady friend. (Hey, what girl doesn't like chocolate?) Once you've made it, it will be a favourite of yours as well—and maybe you'll get a second date!

CORY'S TIPS

» Be sure to use a good-quality dark chocolate (75% cocoa or higher).
» Keep the stems on the pears for easier handling and only dip them halfway into the melted chocolate for a nicer presentation.

8 cups (2 L) water
3 cups (750 mL) dry white wine
½ cup (125 mL) honey
1 Tbsp (15 mL) lemon juice
1 Tbsp (15 mL) fresh orange juice
4 cardamom pods
2 star anise
½ tsp (2 mL) black peppercorns
½ tsp (2 mL) cloves
1 bay leaf
6 Bartlett pears, peeled
½ lb (250 g) rich dark chocolate
½ cup (125 mL) sliced toasted almonds

Place a large deep saucepan over medium-high heat and add the water, wine, honey, citrus juices, cardamom, star anise, peppercorns, cloves, and bay leaf. Gently place the peeled pears in the liquid and bring to a boil. Reduce the heat to a low simmer and cook the pears until fork tender, about 20 minutes.

Gently transfer the pears to a large mixing bowl. Using a metal strainer, pour enough of the poaching liquid over pears to just cover them. Cover the bowl with plastic wrap and refrigerate until cool, about 2 hours.

Place a medium saucepan over medium-high heat and add the remaining strained poaching liquid. Bring the liquid to a boil and cook until it's thick enough to coat the back of a spoon. Refrigerate until serving time.

Melt the chocolate until smooth in the top of a double boiler over simmering water, about 5 minutes. Line a large, rimmed baking sheet with parchment paper and spread the toasted almonds over it. Dip the pears in the melted chocolate and then roll them in the toasted almonds. Transfer to a large plate and refrigerate until the chocolate is set, about 20 minutes. Serve with a light drizzle of reduced poaching liquid and a glass of your favourite ice wine.

Serves 8
Prep time: 25 minutes
Cook time: none

SUNDAY BRUNCH FRUIT SALAD

If you serve this dish at a family gathering, keep an eye on the little ones, because there is some alcohol content. I remember attending my grandparents' anniversary celebration and sampling a fruit salad similar to this one. I managed to have several servings and became quite intoxicated! I was already a pretty rambunctious kid, and adding alcohol and multiple bowls of fruit made me downright crazy. Catch me if you can!

CORY'S TIPS

» Any combination of fresh, ripe fruits will work well in this fruit salad.

» To supreme grapefruit or any citrus fruit, remove the skin of each section with a sharp paring knife.

½ honeydew melon, seeded and chopped

½ cantaloupe, seeded and chopped

½ seedless watermelon, chopped

1 quart (1 L) fresh strawberries, stemmed and halved

2 cups (500 mL) washed and halved grapes

1 grapefruit, peeled, sectioned, and supremed (see Tip)

2 bananas, sliced

2 peaches, peeled, pitted, and sliced

½ pineapple, peeled, cored, and chopped

1 quart (1 L) fresh blueberries

¼ cup (60 mL) amaretto liqueur

2 cups (500 mL) Champagne or sparkling wine

Combine all the fruit in a large bowl and stir in the amaretto. Cover and refrigerate for 1 hour to macerate. Divide the fruit among eight small serving bowls. Top each with Champagne and enjoy with friends!

Serves 4
Prep time: 5 minutes
Cook time: none

VANILLA-BALSAMIC SUNDAE

Balsamic vinegar with ice cream? Yes, you read that right. When you serve this to your guests, have a little fun with them and see if they can guess what's on it before they taste it. I've heard chocolate sauce to cherry sauce and everything in between, but no one has gotten it right yet. This dessert may seem simple, and it is, but the flavours are complex and very delicious.

CORY'S TIP
» Be sure to use high-quality, aged balsamic vinegar for the best results.

8 scoops vanilla ice cream
3 Tbsp (45 mL) balsamic vinegar

Place two scoops of ice cream in each bowl. Drizzle 2 tsp (10 mL) of balsamic vinegar over each serving. Enjoy!

Serves 4
Prep time: 5 minutes
Cook time: none

PAPAYA & LIME

When I was a child, some of my European friends would have sweets for breakfast, as it was customary in their culture. I always wanted to have dessert for breakfast but I was not allowed. Now it's possible with this simple dessert that is all-natural and so tasty.

2 papayas, seeded and halved
¼ cup (60 mL) lime juice

Score the papayas in a crisscross fashion, making many cuts. Drizzle 1 Tbsp (15 mL) of lime juice over each half and eat immediately!

CORY'S TIPS

» Perfectly ripe papaya is essential for this simple dish. If you don't know how to judge ripeness, ask the produce manager at your local store, or simply look for lots of yellow and red colour on the skin. The skin should give a little under firm pressure.

» Be sure to wash all fruits before using, to remove pesticide residues.

Makes 20 large cookies
Prep time: 20 minutes
Cook time: 15 minutes

HOT CHOCOLATE CHIP COOKIES

Years ago, I began making my own dark chocolates with fresh cayenne chilies, and they were an instant hit. That got me thinking: *Shouldn't there be a chocolate chip cookie with chilies too?* Now there is, and it's a good thing that this recipe makes 20 big cookies because it only burns when you stop eating them. I recommend serving them with a glass of milk.

CORY'S TIP

» Chili and chocolate are great partners in both sweet and savoury dishes. If you don't want these really hot, experiment with the amount of chili.

½ cup (125 mL) butter, softened
½ cup (125 mL) brown sugar
1 egg
¾ tsp (4 mL) pure vanilla extract
1¼ cups (310 mL) all-purpose flour
½ tsp (2 mL) sea salt
½ tsp (2 mL) baking soda
1 fresh red cayenne chili, seeded and finely chopped
1 cup (250 mL) semi-sweet chocolate chips
½ cup (125 mL) chopped nuts

Preheat the oven to 375°F (190°C). In a large mixing bowl, cream the butter, sugar, egg, and vanilla, beating until light and smooth. In a separate large mixing bowl combine the flour, salt, baking soda, and chopped chili. Stir in the chocolate chips and nuts, and thoroughly mix into the egg and butter mixture. Drop the mixture by spoonfuls on 2 large ungreased baking sheets and bake in the centre of the oven for 10 to 12 minutes. Remove from the pan and allow to cool on a rack.

Makes 2 cups (500 mL)
Prep time: 15 minutes
Cook time: 1 hour

CORY'S KICKIN' CAYENNE COCOA-COATED PECANS

These are a wonderful little dessert snack and can be used in combination with many other dishes. Scatter them over salads, serve them on ice cream, and add them to Hot Chocolate Chip Cookies (page 161). If some people find them too spicy, there's more for you!

2 Tbsp (30 mL) butter
½ tsp (2 mL) ground cinnamon
½ tsp (2 mL) ground cayenne
¼ tsp (1 mL) ground nutmeg
2 cups (500 mL) halved pecans
2 Tbsp (30 mL) raw cane sugar
1 Tbsp (15 mL) unsweetened cocoa powder

Preheat the oven to 250°F (120°C). Place a small saucepan over low heat and add the butter, cinnamon, cayenne, and nutmeg. Whisk to combine. Add the pecans and sprinkle with the sugar. Pour the mixture onto a large, rimmed baking sheet and bake in the centre of the oven until golden in colour, about 1 hour. Stir the mixture every 20 minutes.

Sift the cocoa powder over the hot pecans and let cool on the pan. Enjoy as a snack or as a treat with ice cream.

CORY'S TIPS

» Raw cane sugar (sometimes labelled turbinado-style sugar) is available in the baking aisle of most grocery stores. It is a healthier alternative to processed white sugar, and adds a rich flavour. There are different levels of coarseness, but I find the medium works best for cooking and baking.

» Store the nuts in an airtight container in your freezer and they will last for months.

Makes 6 servings
Prep time: 15 minutes
Cook time: 1 hour

CORY'S CANE SUGAR CRÈME BRÛLÉE

A close friend of mine with an allergy to lactose never wants to miss out on dessert, so I have experimented with making this dessert for people with lactose intolerance. Not an easy thing to do, although I have recently had success with lactose-free milk. (I would like to take this opportunity to apologize to French chefs everywhere.) You can experiment for yourself, but this (it goes without saying) is the traditional version.

CORY'S TIPS

» Add 3 fl oz (90 mL) of Baileys Irish Cream to your scalded cream for an original twist on this dish.

» If you are unable to locate fresh vanilla beans, substitute 1 Tbsp (15 mL) pure vanilla extract.

» Raw cane sugar is sometimes called turbinado-style sugar.

» When I prepare this dessert, I like to save the egg whites to make a healthy omelette the next morning.

2 cups (500 mL) light cream or half-and-half
2 fresh vanilla bean pods, split lengthwise
8 egg yolks
½ cup (125 mL) raw cane sugar

Place a medium saucepan over medium heat and add the cream and vanilla beans. Scald the cream for 2 minutes (don't allow it to come to a boil) and remove from the heat. Remove the vanilla.

Preheat the oven to 300°F (150°C). In a large bowl, combine the egg yolks and ¼ cup (60 mL) of the sugar, whisking until smooth. Add the scalded cream very slowly to the egg mixture, whisking continuously. Pour the mixture into six ovenproof ramekins and place in a 10- × 15-inch (4 L) casserole dish. Using a kettle, carefully pour boiling water into the casserole dish to create a water bath that comes halfway up the sides of the ramekins. Transfer to the centre rack of the oven and bake for 45 to 50 minutes.

Remove from the hot water bath and refrigerate until completely chilled. Sprinkle the remaining ¼ cup (60 mL) sugar evenly overtop each ramekin. Use a blowtorch, or place under the broiler, to melt the sugar until caramelized and golden.

Makes one loaf
Prep time: 15 minutes
Cook time: 1 hour

OLD-FASHIONED BANANA BREAD

I was given this recipe by my friend Michelle. I love it so much I had to include it here. (The really great part is the addition of chocolate chips!) I never like to throw away food, and this is a wonderful opportunity to make even overripe bananas a delicious delectable. Thanks, Michelle!

CORY'S TIPS

» This is another great opportunity to use Cory's Kickin' Cayenne Cocoa-Coated Pecans (page 162). Substitute them for the walnuts.

» If you can't use up overripe bananas right away, peel them, slice them lengthwise, and freeze them in a large freezer bag for later use.

½ cup (125 mL) butter, softened
½ cup (125 mL) brown sugar
½ cup (125 mL) white sugar
2 eggs
1¾ cups (435 mL) all-purpose flour
1 tsp (5 mL) baking soda
½ tsp (2 mL) baking powder
½ tsp (2 mL) sea salt
2 very ripe bananas, mashed
½ cup (125 mL) semi-sweet chocolate chips
½ cup (125 mL) chopped walnuts

Preheat the oven to 350°F (180°C). Lightly grease a 10- × 6-inch (3 L) loaf pan. Combine the butter, both sugars, and eggs in a large bowl, mixing well. Sift the flour, baking soda, baking powder, and salt into the bowl and mix well to combine. Stir in the bananas, chocolate chips, and walnuts.

Transfer the batter to the loaf pan and place in the centre of the oven. Bake for 1 hour or until a toothpick inserted in the centre comes out clean. Remove from the oven and allow to cool in the pan for 20 minutes before turning out onto a rack. Wrap any leftover portion with plastic wrap and store in the freezer, as it keeps very well.

Index

Acknowledgements

Without the encouragement and support of key people, my journey would have presented far greater difficulties. I believe that we are all in charge of our own destiny and must take responsibility for ourselves and our actions. I have had to accept that my injury was the result of my own doing and that I have no one to blame except myself. But I do not blame myself for my injury; I prefer to see it as a very powerful lesson. It may sound crazy to some, but in many ways I feel my life is fuller, more complete, and happier than before. In fact, it sounds a little crazy to me, too! But it's the truth.

My goal is to motivate and inspire others through this book and my heartfelt words. I want to acknowledge the support and help of the people who surround me; they deserve recognition and should share in my success as if it were their own, for they are all an important part of it.

This is my opportunity to repay these amazing people, by sharing what they have given to me with others who endeavour to achieve their dreams. Thank you all so very much!

Whitecap Books, for the opportunity of a lifetime! And **Robert McCullough**, for taking a chance and believing in me. **Frederic Robinson** of FPR Productions (www.fprproductions.com) for your support, encouragement, and hard work. **Gavin Wilding**, for helping to make a dream come true. **Tracey Emerick** and **Mark Hutzler**, of the Marco Polo group (www.themarcopologroup.com), for your time, patience, and wonderful energy.

Christyna Melnyk, for your friendship and for introducing me to Salt of Life (www.saltoflife.ca). **Lance Sullivan** of Concept Photography (www.conceptphoto.ca) and **Rainer Plendl**, for your fantastic photographic and styling skills, and for making me look good! **Dawn Tyndall**, for your positive support and educational information. **Jason Jones**, for being the brother I never had but always wanted. **Mairi and Marty Dunn**, for your love and support, and for putting up with me! **Jason Pope**, for being a great friend, a wonderful support, and a terrific inspiration. **Ryan Riddle** and **Hilary Malone**: without you my kitchen would still be a mess. **Natalie Mitchell**: foxy danger! What else can I say? Thanks for everything. My father, **Wray Parsons**, and his wife, **Dorothy Parsons**, for your love and support, and for instilling in me all of your greatest attributes. My mother, **Carol Bertram**, for your love and support; none of this would've been possible without you. **Mike and Danielle Southwell**, for your culinary influence and friendship. **Mike and Jen Dilfer**, for a great way to use late-summer zucchini squash. **Faith Leather**, for your wonderful apple crisp recipe. **Michelle Wilson**, for the best banana bread recipe in the world. **David Gilks**, for your health and wellness expertise and continuing support. **Marlon Brown**, because you're the nicest guy I've ever met. **Flying Fish**, for your amazing and selfless support. **Sandra Dunn** of West Coast Floral, for your flower arrangements—they're the best. **Thrifty Foods**, for supporting the Cory Parsons Project. **Darren Kiedyk** and staff at **Urban Beet Food Co.** (www.urbanbeet.ca), for your support and encouragment. **Dan Caron**: now I know how you keep your chef's jacket so clean.

And to **my readers**, for taking an interest in this cookbook.